Battleground Europe
EPEHY

Battleground Europe

EPEHY

K W Mitchinson

Series editor
Nigel Cave

LEO COOPER

First published in 1998 by
LEO COOPER
190 Shaftesbury Avenue, London WC2H 8JL
an imprint of
Pen Sword Books Limited
47 Church Street, Barnsley, South Yorkshire S70 2AS

ISBN 0 85052 627 2

A CIP catalogue of this book is available
from the British Library

Printed by Redwood Books Limited
Trowbridge, Wiltshire

For up-to-date information on other titles produced under the Leo Cooper imprint,
please telephone or write to:
Pen & Sword Books Ltd, FREEPOST, 47 Church Street
Barnsley, South Yorkshire S70 2AS
Telephone 01226 734222

CONTENTS

Germans in Gonnelieu inspect the remains of British 6 inch 26 cwt Howitzer. March/April 1918.

INTRODUCTION BY
SERIES EDITOR

The village of Epéhy is one of the focal point for much of the activity of the British Army when it made its advance to the Hindenburg Line in April 1917. With the popular concentration upon the Somme battlefields, there is a strong tendency to forget that the British troops spent the equivalent of a year or so in positions before the immensely fortified German line. It was during these months that much of the technological and tactical developments of the war took place, encompassing as they did the British advance, the Cambrai battle to the north, the German spring offensive and the British riposte, part of the 'Hundred Days'.

Bill Mitchinson's work is an excellent introduction to an area which saw Allied troops from Britain, Australia and America all playing their part in the ferociously fought battles in this open part of the French countryside, on the limits of the Somme département. There still remain the physical reminders of the war, chunks of concrete, isolated British cemeteries, the American Somme cemetery at Bony, as well as residues of fortifications in the canal tunnel under Bellicourt and Bony. It is not difficult to see the vast change in both offensive and defensive tactics between the fighting here and that which had characterised much of what went on at the Somme, especially in the early stages. Yet there seems to me to be a disinclination from many interested observers, especially in the United Kingdom, to take any great interest in the fighting in these later stages of the war. A notable exception to this rule is Martin Middlebrooke's excellent book, *The Kaiser's Battle,* which is readily available and one I would strongly recommend. One can but hope that visitors to this area, now they have a number of guides available, will seek further information on this phase of the conflict.

On a personal note, Epéhy is of particular family significance to me. At the time of the German March attack my grandfather was serving as the RQMS of 7/Leicesters. Just before the attack he had been granted leave, and when the blow fell was awaiting the boat for England. Needless to say, his few days at home in Leicester were promptly cancelled. His battalion – indeed his brigade, the 110th (Leicestershire) – did notably well in those early days of fighting, but his absence quite probably saved his life. Another chapter of accidents ensured that he was returned to his unit, for as part of a composite battalion rushed up to stem the German flow, he happened to pass his own battalion coming the other way and was immediately commandeered back to his own battalion. Of such chances of fate are the lives of individuals and the future settled

Nigel Cave, Ely Place.

**The area covered by this book
is inside the white lines.**

━ ━ Staring Line • • • • **Main Hindenburg Line**

ATTACK ON HINDENBURG LINE, 18 SEPT 1918

INTRODUCTION

The villages and fields around Epéhy are infrequently visited by British tourists to the Western Front. They do not have the emotional appeal of Ypres or the Somme and many Britons who regularly make trips to the Front have little or no idea of their historical significance. This is a great shame as there are several memorials, concrete emplacements and many cemeteries scattered around the area. The motorway has carved its way through the fields to the east but, in general, it remains an area of natural beauty. It has not suffered from the commercialisation which has done so much to destroy the atmosphere and calm of the Somme. There are no coachloads of disinterested, litter-strewing school children and their harassed minders, nor are there tourist cafés and gift shops. There is an abundance of open space, easy walking and peace.

The war did little physical damage to the area until 1917. The German retreat to the Hindenburg Line in March and April gave British forces access to Epéhy for the first time since August 1914. British attempts to gain observation over the Hindenburg Line resulted in several important engagements during the summer of 1917, while the German counter-attack during the Battle of Cambrai, also affected the land to the east and north of Epéhy. However, the most significant

Ruins of Peronne after the German retreat to the Hindenburg line. The notice left by the Germans reads, 'Don't be angry, but only admire'.

action took place in the Forward and Battle Zones of Fifth Army in March 1918 and against the Hindenburg defences in the following September. The area is therefore of crucial importance to a wider understanding of the Allied disasters and victories of the final year of the war.

By car, visitors can reach the area from their more usual wanderings on the Somme within 40 minutes. There are plenty of reasonable hotels in Péronne, Cambrai and St Quentin, but most Britons can just as easily use their normal accommodation in Albert and its surrounds and drive across to Epéhy for the day. The ideal means of discovering the area is by either foot or mountain bike. It is for these travellers that this and its companion books on Riqueval and Villers Plouich are primarily written. There are no fences to bar your way and, providing you use intelligence and consideration, you will offend no-one. Like the Somme, the area can also be driven. There are places to park in most villages and tractors tend to keep to the network of headlands rather than the roads. But, sitting behind the wheel and giving an occasional glance to the sides, reveals little of the character of any region.

Epéhy is a village and area which deserve exploration; the countryside is beautiful and the farmers helpful. The fields and woods are again part of a working environment. For the sake of those who depend upon them for their livelihood, enjoy and respect them.

ACKNOWLEDGEMENTS

The information contained within these pages comes from many years of walking and cycling the area, and from a variety of primary and secondary sources. The principal documented sources are the war diaries of the units which fought in the village and its surrounds. The detail found within those volumes has been supplemented by that taken from divisional, regimental and battalion histories and from personal reminiscences.

Books of the Battleground series are not intended to be academic studies. Consequently, I have followed the now established tradition of referencing only direct quotations. The bibliography at the rear gives many of the more easily accessible secondary sources consulted in the preparation of the book. Several major reference libraries hold some of the volumes, but the collection held by the Department of Printed Books at the Imperial War Museum is probably unparalleled. Over four dozen unit war diaries were used and, as their PRO War Office classification numbers are easy to acquire, they have not been listed in the bibliography.

I extend my grateful thanks to the staffs of the Public Record Office and the IWM's Departments of Photographs and Printed Books. Mrs Mary Bayliss and her colleagues have, as usual, been of immense help and encouragement. The Trustees of both archives have granted permission to use material taken from their collections. My thanks also to the ladies of Accrington Library. Their collection of Commonwealth War Graves Commission registers has been of great use and their kindness has been much appreciated. Several individuals, in particular Nigel Cave, Kevin Kelly, David Key and Peter Oldham have given of their expertise and made constructive criticism. I also offer thanks to the many French farmers and labourers who over the years have shown such tolerance at my halting French. Finally, special thanks to my frequent travelling and walking companion JB.

GENERAL ADVICE

The village of Epéhy lies at the heart of this book and at the heart of an agricultural region. Before you leave for the Front, familiarise yourself with the general lie of the land and the position of the principal sites covered in the tours. Preparation in the weeks before a trip makes the actual event so much more rewarding. Pore over your IGN Green Series and trench maps to identify paths, tracks, posts, cemeteries and roads. Remember, the designated number of French roads usually change when they cross department boundaries.

Although many British visitors have heard of the Battle of Epéhy, few know much about it. For that reason there is rather more military detail about the events of 1917-1918 than is commonly found in other books in the series. It remains small enough to fit into a pocket so take it with you when you go. By providing the military detail, a description of what can be seen in the area today and a suggested tour, each chapter is designed to stand on its own. Cemeteries are arranged alphabetically at the end of the book. This appendix also lists some of the cemeteries a little to the rear of the areas covered in the book. Many of them will be passed or reached by a short diversion when driving to Epéhy. Figures in bold print in the text refer to points of interest marked on the relevant tour map.

The best time for investigating the land and the physical remains is during the early spring or late autumn. The crops are low or recently harvested and the fields passable. Only walk on the fields when absolutely necessary; keep to the edge and never go on if there are crops growing. The baulks, tracks and headlands are sufficient to allow interesting explorations without the need to offend the local farmers. Wear sensible shoes or boots, wear trousers rather than shorts, take a waterproof, sun cream, a compass and a stick. The latter is for prodding through undergrowth rather than defending yourself against roaming dogs. Fortunately, French dogs tend to be less aggressive and more under control than their Belgian cousins. Also acquire some liquid and solid sustenance before leaving your hotel. Epéhy has a couple of cafés and several shops, but most places close between noon and 2.00pm.

If travelling by car, do not be tempted to persevere too far down what appear to be encouragingly suitable tracks. Many just end, while others progressively degenerate into little more than vague grass paths. You might see a stalwart Renault 4 forcing its way through, but it does not have to take broken half-shafts back up to the coast. Do not park on the side of the road. There is so little traffic about that there are always places by the village church or Mairie. Mountain bikers will find the routes less than demanding, but interesting. Nevertheless, carry the usual spare inner tube, pump and spanners. All visitors should carry their E111 and take the usual anti-tetanus precautions.

Finally, a warning. When walking the area in autumn or winter, be very wary of the French weekend 'hunter'. He is an exceptionally irresponsible individual who will merrily blast away at anything that moves. His concept of safety is barely developed and 12-bore pellets can whistle uncomfortably close to your head. If you remonstrate and point out that you have an aversion to being peppered by buckshot, he will merely shrug his shoulders or claim not to understand Anglo-Saxon.

MAPS

Most British tourists to the Somme carry the Michelin 1:200000 No.53 as their essential companion. The same map also covers the area around Epéhy. This map is perfectly adequate for the driver and casual wanderer. The IGN series of 1:25000 gives a much better coverage, but for the really interested walker or cyclist, the 1:10000 trench maps are essential. These maps can be purchased from the IWM's Department of Printed Books and the Western Front Association. A pedometer or mileometer ('on board computers' to the *cognoscenti*) are useful additions to your equipment.

This volume includes extracts from some of the official trench maps and hand drawn 'tour maps'. These vary in scale but have the same symbols. Modern road numbers and cemeteries have been included in order to aid orientation. Village and place names have been spelt in the manner used by the army. This does not always coincide with the present-day spelling. Dotted lines indicate tracks and paths which, as a general rule, should not be driven. This is not to say that they are impassable at all times of the year, but many are grass headlands rather than conventional farm tracks. Understandably, farmers do not appreciate British cars marauding across their fields. There is also the distinct possibility of getting bogged down or grounding exhausts.

The 'tour maps' give an indication of the distance and an idea of the time taken to walk the route. If they seem a little ambitious, they can easily be shortened or amended. Much depends upon how long you spend in the cemeteries or take over eating your picnic. Just use your common sense. The area has some splendid views and awaits discovery by British visitors.

Key for 'Tour Maps'

†	Crucifix
⊠	Cemetery
(wood symbol)	Wood
++++++++	Railway
▬▬▬	Motorway
────	Route Nationale
────	'D' Roads
- - - - -	Not suitable for cars
P	Parking

PRELUDE

On 23 February 1917, battalions of 55 Brigade, 18th Division, reported that they were in possession of enemy trenches near Petit Miraumont on the Ancre. The Germans had apparently gone, leaving behind a few fires burning in deserted dugouts. Later that day similar reports from other sections of Fifth Army's front arrived at Divisional and later Army HQ. By the following day it was evident that a major German withdrawal from their forward positions was in progress. Huge fires were seen burning in what had been the German rear areas. Cautious patrols reported that the enemy was gone, but that he had left behind a variety of booby traps and a zone which showed signs of deliberate and wanton devastation. As the news spread along the front, a young, somewhat idealistic subaltern of the 8/Warwick rejoiced at what he thought was the beginning of an inglorious retreat by the Kaiser's army. His platoon was less enthusiastic. True, there might be opportunities to pick up the odd souvenir or two, but to Edwin Vaughan's men, it meant merely 'more ... marching'.[1]

What was by no means clear at the time was how far the Germans would withdraw or whether the tactic was simply a ruse to lure on the Allied armies before launching a surprise counter-stroke. The existence behind the Somme front of three reserve lines of defence, five to six miles in depth, was well-known to British Intelligence; it

The flooded valley of the Ancre in the Miraumont area, which fell in March 1917 during the German retreat. TAYLOR LIBRARY

was initially assumed that the enemy would make a fighting withdrawal to these prepared positions and then halt. However, it was also known that further to the rear another zone of deep defences was under construction and, in places, nearing completion. It seemed possible the withdrawal would perhaps continue until the enemy reached what the British had christened the Hindenburg Line but which to the Germans was the *Siegfried Stellung.*

Construction of this new position, which was eventually to stretch from Arras to the Aisne, had begun in late September 1916. In October RFC pilots reported recent excavations near Quéant but it was not until early 1917 that stories from French agents, an escaped Russian prisoner of war and others suggested there was something major going on. The winter weather and German air supremacy prevented any reliable aerial reconnaissance but it gradually became clear that the Germans were employing large numbers of civilians and captured Russians to dig and build a series of strong defences. It was in fact only on the day following the German withdrawal opposite 55 Brigade that the course and extent of the Hindenburg Line facing the BEF became apparent; even then its extreme southern end in front of the French remained shrouded in uncertainty.

The decision to build the *Siegfried Stellung* had in the first instance been taken as a precautionary measure, an insurance policy in case the battle of attrition on the Somme front became too much of a drain on the resources of the Imperial Army. Even when the decision had been made and construction begun, there was no certainty that it would eventually be occupied by a voluntary withdrawal. In the event of pressure on the Somme becoming too severe the line might be utilised as a system against which British forces would wear themselves down in repeated assaults, but the German High Command kept an open mind as to how or when it might be used. Even if a decision was made to withdraw voluntarily to the new system, Ludendorff had certainly not abandoned any plan which might involve his forces turning about and delivering a bloody

Ludendorff, who was made First Quartermaster-General of the German army under Hindenburg in 1916.

riposte to the pursuing armies.

Strategically and tactically, although perhaps not morally, a withdrawal in early 1917 made sense to the German army. Tied down in the east and west and unsure of the resolve of her allies, Germany was incapable of launching any large-scale offensive. The anticipated 75 Allied divisions could be faced by only 40 German ones. If a withdrawal was effected Ludendorff could eliminate two dangerous salients in his line, shorten his front by 25 miles and save perhaps 14 divisions in the process. Secure behind these formidable defences his army could resist any Allied onslaught and wait until the U-boat campaign of unrestricted sinkings compelled the British to open peace talks. If this was to be the object of the line, its defences would have to be sufficiently strong to ward off British and French assaults for an anticipated 12 months. Not surprisingly therefore, the Hindenburg Line was designed to be impregnable.

There was disagreement within the German High Command over the positioning and design of the zonal defences, but along most of its length it consisted of an outpost line, a battle zone and a rear zone. Typically, the outpost line was some 600m deep, sited on the crest of hills, protected by wire and manned by squads armed with personal weapons and light machine guns. Behind it on the reverse slope was the battle zone. This usually consisted of three belts of wire, each 10–15m deep, in front of an extensive array of concrete machine-gun posts. These were sited to cover both each other and the re-entrant angle of the zig-zag wire belts. Fire trenches often contained concrete dugouts capable of sheltering the defenders during bombardments. The battle zone was connected by deeply buried cable and communication trenches to the rear zone. Here, concrete artillery observation posts, with views over the top of the infantry pill boxes and fire trenches, were in contact with batteries further back. Light railways supplied ammunition to the guns, and trench stores and equipment often to within a few metres of the front positions.[2]

Crown Prince Rupprecht

January's fighting on the Somme front and the appalling misery endured by troops on both sides convinced Crown Prince Rupprecht that *First Army* could not take much more. Continuous British pressure

15

Trees deliberately felled by the retreating Germans, a policy to which Ruppprecht had strongly objected.

north and south of the Ancre was endangering German morale, so on 28 January Rupprecht demanded that a voluntary withdrawal to the new lines be authorised; on 4 February Wilhelm signed the directive. The prepared plan allowed for 35 so-called 'Alberich days' - the period during which all the administrative and support units would withdraw and the land between the existing front and the new line laid waste. From 16 March, depending on how far behind the front positions the *Stellung* was, between two and four 'marching days' were allowed for the bulk of the fighting troops to take their positions in the zone.

So convinced was Rupprecht of the necessity of an immediate withdrawal, that he ordered his forces on the Ancre front to commence their march to the rear on the night of 22-23 February. He was less

General Rawlinson, GOC Fourth Army.

convinced however of the manner in which the withdrawal was to be made. Rupprecht had objected to a scorched earth policy and had even threatened to resign his command in protest. He was persuaded to stay for internal political reasons, but his abhorrence of the policy, which he considered to be a stain on the honour of the German army, remained. There were also practical considerations; the deliberate destruction of houses and other buildings would provide the pursuing forces with readily available road-mending and crater-filling materials. Rupprecht's objections were however over-ruled, and the destruction began. General Rawlinson, GOC Fourth Army, decided to adopt a cautious policy of pursuit. His army held positions north and south of the meandering Somme, the centre of his command lying roughly astride the Amiens-St Quentin road, four miles west of Péronne. The Hindenburg Line lay approximately 12 miles east of Péronne. His army would have to cover a greater distance than Fifth Army on his left; indeed his right flank division would have almost double the mileage compared to that of his left. Rawlinson had thus no reason to conduct a swift pursuit. He knew that getting his forces across the Somme Canal, river and marshes about Péronne would prove a major problem; so too would the bridging of the unfinished Canal du Nord north of Péronne. As several of his reserve divisions had already been ear-marked for operations elsewhere, Rawlinson was unsure of how much strength he might have to deploy. Even when he reached the *Stellung* he realised Fourth Army would be in no position to attack it. Until sufficient artillery (and Fourth Army was already very short of heavy guns) was within range and adequately supplied, no significant operation could be authorised. The urgency and vigour of the chase would therefore be dictated by conditions prevailing in the devastated zone and the speed with which their challenge could be overcome. Fortunately, at least for the time being, his army, unlike Gough's Fifth, was not required to conduct a vigorous pursuit in order to support Third Army's imminent offensive at Arras.

By 18 March, the last 'marching day', the main body of German troops opposite Fourth Army was scheduled to be ensconced in and

The destruction of Peronne by the Germans before their retreat.

behind the Hindenburg Line. On the previous day, and several miles to the west, one company of the 8/Warwick, 48th(South Midland) Division, crossed the deep trench of the Somme Canal by bridge and was ferried across the marshes by raft into Péronne. Here the Warwicks witnessed for the first time the effects of the German policy of deliberate destruction in a town of substantial size. In pre-war days wealthy merchants from Amiens and Paris had retired to Péronne and built substantial houses overlooking the river. The French government prohibited the friendly shelling of several historic towns and cities, Péronne being one example, so until the German withdrawal it had suffered very little damage. Now the houses and shops had their fronts blown out and the cathedral was almost totally destroyed. Delayed-action devices exploded as British troops cautiously explored the ruins. When the devastation was witnessed by one officer of the 10/Manchester, it prompted him to write:

> *'The sights we see around us condemn* [the Germans] *to extreme perdition and though an Englishman is not given to hating it would be a great sin if the Bosch were not classed as swine by Englishmen for many generations to come'.*[3]

The Warwicks' entry to Péronne had been the result of some exceptional work by the divisional RE and Pioneers. The first bridge over the canal was erected and open to traffic in only eight hours and in the course of the next ten days, ten further bridges over the canal and the marshes were constructed within the divisional area.

Leaving Péronne to the support and service troops, III Corps moved on. Major-General Fanshaw, known as the 'chocolate soldier' on account of his habit of distributing chocolate to the troops, was in temporary command of the corps. In order to keep in contact with the enemy and to keep his rearguards under pressure, Fanshaw created an advanced guard comprised of the 4/Ox & Bucks, the corps cavalry and cyclists, two sections of RE and two batteries of field artillery.[4] Followed by other units of III Corps, this force moved east and north-east from Péronne. Within two days of its formation the corps cavalry horses were exhausted by the hock-deep mud, a lack of fodder and by over-use; they were replaced by units of the 5th Cavalry Division on 24 March. Two days later, one company of the Ox & Bucks, two squadrons of the 18/Lancers and two armoured cars captured Roisel, the garrison of this small town having largely run away when the armoured cars approached. Its capture was important as the town was a railway junction and, once secured, the broad gauge line could be relaid to connect with the track already being pushed across the

Cavalry crossing a temporary bridge. TAYLOR LIBRARY

devastated zone from Péronne. Communications and supply remained seemingly insurmountable problems. Each corps was forced to employ at least a division of troops it could ill-afford on road-making. The Territorials of the 59th and 61st Divisions, for example, spent most of March behind the advance, labouring incessantly to clear and improve roads and communications. At first, everything was brought forward by horse transport but in time, light and standard gauge railways would traverse the new zone of occupation and convoys of lorries would career along its relaid roads; for now, the army relied almost exclusively on horses, mules and infantry.

German rearguards of between 50–100 men were left in most villages and in many of the nearby copses. The tactic developed by the 5th Cavalry Division and the Canadian Cavalry Brigade was to send an armoured car up the road towards a village to draw fire while the cavalry galloped in from the flanks and the infantry followed up. This worked well on many occasions and in many villages. The Fort Garry Horse took Ytres after a sharp fight and noted:

> *'This is the first village taken by British cavalry since October 1914'.*[5]

On 27 March the Ambala and Canadian Brigades were ordered to take Guyencourt, Saulcourt and Villers-Faucon. The Royal Canadian Dragoons had occupied Longavesnes the previous day and early on the 27th took Liéramont. They were then supposed to lead the attack on Saulcourt. However, the Dragoons could not disengage so it fell to the Fort Gary Horse to attack the village. A bombardment of 45 minutes fired by the Royal Canadian Horse Artillery preceded the attack in which the Fort Garry swept through the village and established outposts within 500m of Epéhy. At night the infantry came up to relieve them and the outposts were for the time being abandoned.

To the left, Lord Strathcona's Horse assaulted Guyencourt. The regiment had taken Equancourt on the 23rd and, although it had lost only four men wounded, nine horses had been killed or destroyed. Following the brief bombardment, and in a howling snow storm, they moved up the slope towards Guyencourt. Enemy shells began to fall among the horses and then, when they came to within 1000m of the village, machine guns opened up. Several saddles were empty by the time the lead squadrons reached the shelter of a valley in front of the houses. The troopers dismounted and fixed bayonets. At this critical moment:

> *...when the enemy showed no intention whatever of retiring and the fire was still intense, Lieutenant Frederick Harvey, who was in command of the leading troop, ran forward well ahead of his men, dashed at the trench still fully manned, jumped the wire, shot the gunner and captured the machine gun.*[6]

Lt. Frederick Harvey

Harvey's men followed him over the wire and into the trench. The enemy fled, 'casting away all their equipment' and did not stay to defend the village itself. German cavalry were seen in the background, but they too apparently 'beat it as fast as they could'.[7] Harvey was awarded the VC for his exploit.

Meanwhile, to the south of the Canadians the Ambala Brigade attacked Villers-Faucon. Two armoured cars approached on the Longavesnes road while two squadrons of the 8/Hussars worked around the flanks. Both armoured cars were put out of action while still 200m from the village – German armour-piercing bullets made their first impressive debut – but the cavalry under the command of Major Van der Byl charged forward and took the village at a cost of two dead and fourteen wounded. The Hussars occupied the village until a company of the 8/Warwicks came up to relieve them. Snow lay along the roads and across the fields over which the infantry trudged in the wake of the cavalry. On his way up from Longavesnes

Vaughan came across Indian Lancers huddled around braziers and chattering with cold. Inside the village he discovered a Hussar behaving like a idiot and what he described as a 'windy' major boasting of their courage in taking the place.[8] Courage was shown in abundance by the King George's Own Lancers the following day when they galloped across the basin between Ste Emilie and Epéhy, coming under intense shrapnel and machine-gun fire. The Hussars surged on until balked by uncut wire. An officer of the regiment thought that on the whole the enemy's

'rifle fire was bad...the country was very open and almost ideal for cavalry but the weather was very unfavourable'.[9]

Their animals too suffered grievously from the snow; on the following day, with the horses near to collapse from exposure and exhaustion, the 5th Cavalry Division was withdrawn.

The closer the British divisions drew to the Hindenburg Line, the stiffer became the German resistance. Parts of the line were not yet complete so enemy rearguards bought time by fighting hard for the outpost villages. German counter-attacks on the 2/Lincoln at Equancourt and the 2/Devon at Aizecourt-le-Bas had served notice of their intention. Furthermore, British forces were coming within range of batteries positioned behind the Hindenburg Line and were encountering a great deal more freshly laid wire. Despite his growing problems of supply and increasing enemy resistance, Haig informed Rawlinson that he would have to quicken the pace of pursuit. French forces on the right of Fourth Army planned to attack the *Stellung* south of St Quentin and required Fourth Army to protect their flank. Rawlinson appreciated the concerns of his French ally but in reality could do little to cover the ground more rapidly. He continued to advance his line of resistance when suitable positions were attained; but this took time. The weather was against him and there was little point in his advance parties forging miles ahead of this line if only to be repulsed or held up by lack of artillery support. His troops were adapting well to open warfare and making good progress, but the capture of each village was no longer a matter of sending in the cavalry and armoured cars. The attacks on Heudicourt, Sorel and Fins illustrate how the advance had by now become a series of set-piece battles.

The three villages lie in a basin, with Heudicourt and Sorel on its southern slopes and Fins in the valley bottom. A horseshoe-shaped northern slope overlooked all three villages. The centre of the 8th Division's outpost line was approximately 1000m south of Sorel; its troops could see easily how the villages were dominated by Dessart

Wood to the west, the hamlet of Révelon to the north (with Genin Well Copses No.1 and 2 alongside) and Jacquenne Copse to the east. On 27 March the Canadian Cavalry Brigade was repulsed when it tried to outflank Sorel and Fins, and at dawn on the 28th a reconnaissance party of seven men of the 2/West Yorks approached to within 200m of German posts in the southern part of Heudicourt before being forced to withdraw. Unfortunately, through what was later described as an

'excess of zeal on the part of some company posts [the patrol] *spent a miserable day in holes between the lines, sniped at by both sides'.*[10]

At dusk on 29 March two patrols from the West Yorks, each of one officer and 15 men, entered Heudicourt and were driven out by concentrated fire. It was apparent that all three villages were strongly held and equally clear that, if they were to be captured and held, the horseshoe would have to be taken as well.

Two infantry brigades, 23 and 25, were detailed for the task. Each was allocated four sections of 18-pounders, one section of 4.5-inch howitzers and 24 machine guns; these were supported by the remainder of the divisional artillery, a brigade of field artillery of the 40th Division and XV Corps cavalry. Two Rifle Brigade battalions of 59 Brigade (20th Division) supported by a Field Company, three batteries and the corps cavalry would attack towards Neuville-Boujonval to protect the left flank of 25 Brigade, while at the same time the artillery of the 48th Division to the right would fire upon the western edges of Peiziere and Epéhy.

At dawn on 30 March 2/RB rushed and took Fins at the same time as the 1/Royal Irish Rifles swept into Sorel. Once the village was secure, the RB put a Battle Patrol Platoon ahead of the battalion on the Fins-Nurlu road with the task of covering the advance of B Company when it emerged from the village to attack Dessart Wood at 4.00pm. At the appointed time and under a good barrage, the company climbed the slope and was met by heavy machine-gun fire. When, however, the enemy realised the strength of the advancing waves, they fled. The wood was secured against little opposition and the company dug in about 200m to its north and east. As soon as the Royal Irish saw the RB had reached the wood, they charged from Sorel, catching on their way many of the Germans fleeing from the RB, and secured the plateau 1500m to the south-east. A squadron of cavalry debouched from Guyencourt, captured Jacquenne Copse and later handed it over to the 2/Scottish Rifles. Having dug in, the RB established contact with their 10th (Service) Battalion to the left.

With part of the horseshoe in friendly hands, 23 Brigade then advanced on Heudicourt. The 2/Devon assembled east of Guyencourt and approached the village from the south-east as the 2/Middlesex advanced from the west. Both battalions kept close behind the barrage and then rushed the village. There was some sharp fighting among the houses and farms but the Devons and Middlesex linked up as planned on the northern side. Fire was directed into the village from German positions at Révelon, Genin Well Copses and from the two or three houses at Railton on the railway east of Heudicourt. The British barrage had already lifted onto Révelon as the Middlesex began climbing the slope to take the hamlet and Genin Well No.1. The Devons, accompanied by corps cavalry, silenced the guns at Railton and then joined with the Middlesex to capture the second copse. At a cost of only 12 dead and 56 wounded the 8th Division had advanced over 6,000m on a three-mile front. A chronicler of the Devon Regiment thought:

> *'The whole operation proved conclusively that trench warfare habits notwithstanding, the 8th Division...had learnt to adapt themselves to the unfamiliar conditions and problems of open warfare'.*[11]

Four days later the 8th Division returned the compliment to the 20th. By attacking Gouzeaucourt Wood and allocating the fire of three batteries to supplement that of the Light Division, the 'old army' assisted its New Army comrades in taking the village of Metz-en-Couture. This 'brilliant'[12] operation, like the attack on Heudicourt, involved a new form of artillery preparation and control and demonstrated that it was not only the regulars who could adapt to open warfare.

Meanwhile, a little to the south-east the Territorials of the 48th

A German wiring party constructing a rough barbed wire defence before retreating to a second line.

Division had taken Ste Emilie. Unlike the operations against Heudicourt and Metz, things did not at first go according to plan. Orders had failed to reach the guns so two companies of the 4/Gloucester attacked the hamlet without artillery support. Having gained a foothold amongst the cottages and repulsed a strong counter-attack, Second Lieutenant Hall's company scrambled into the tangled ruins of the sugar factory and established a Lewis gun in one corner. From among the scattered and broken machinery they could bring under enfilade a machine gun which was preventing the advance of the other company. When the enemy gun was silenced, up to 200 Germans retired on Epéhy, leaving the hamlet and the bodies of their dead comrades in the hands of the Gloucesters.

With the capture of Villers-Faucon, Ste Emilie and Heudicourt there was now really only one ridge remaining between III and XV Corps and the outpost lines of the Hindenburg system. In due course these and other villages would become part of the British defence zone; centres of resistance in case the enemy did sally forth from behind the Stellung. But Fourth Army had not yet achieved its goal. March had seen it pursue the Germans across a wide tract of land laid bare in brutal fashion, fight several quite large engagements and countless smaller ones and strive to keep its forward units supplied with food, ammunition and guns. General Rawlinson's ambition was not merely to take Havrincourt, Trescault, Gonnelieu, Epéhy, Lempire and Hargicourt and then dig in; his staff were already preparing plans to carry the Hindenburg Line between Havrincourt and Banteux. In the event, this ambition was of necessity shelved for seven months and when it was attempted it was not to be Rawlinson's Fourth but Byng's Third Army to whom the task was entrusted. All that however was in the future. First, the final ridge and its villages had to be taken.

Notes

1. E.Vaughan, *Some Desperate Glory*, p.52
2. For a longer discussion on the means and method of the line's construction, see P.Oldham, *The Hindenburg Line.*
3. Letter to his father. Fred Hardman papers, IWM Department of Documents.
4. Its commander was the 48th Division's CRE, Brigadier-General H.Ward. It was subsequently known as Ward's Force.
5. War Diary of the Fort Garry Horse. WO.95.1084
6. War Diary of Lord Strathcona's Horse. WO.95.1085
7. Ibid
8. Vaughan, op.cit. p.70-71
9. War Diary of 18th(KGO)Lancers. WO.95.1164
10. E.Wyrall, *The West Yorkshire Regiment in the Great War,* Vol.II p.29
11. C.Atkinson, *The Devonshire Regiment 1914-1918*, p.239
12. *Annals of the KRRC*, Vol.V p.188

Chapter One

EPEHY

On 31 March 1917 a group of officers from the 48th Division peered through their field glasses at the ruins of Epéhy. The day was overcast and very chilly. Clouds heavy with snow appeared to touch the crest on which the village lay. The valley in front was bereft of cover for any troops approaching the higher ground. As they struggled to discern any feature or landmark upon the ridge, the officers came under fire from heavy guns secreted away in dead ground. Epéhy, although no longer the substantial village it once was, threatened to be a major obstacle on the way to the Hindenburg Line. (See maps on pages 6 and 7)

After a hasty conference at Divisional HQ, it was decided that 144 Brigade, assisted by one battalion of 143 Brigade, should attempt to seize Epéhy in a night attack. At 2.00am on 1 April the 7/Worcester, 6/Gloucester and 6/Warwick crossed the open country in artillery formation. As the first light of a murky dawn spread from the east, the battalions extended and rushed up the slope and into the village. The Germans were taken completely by surprise and in few minutes the enemy troops were either captured or ejected. More substantial

Evidence of the German policy of deliberately destroying the countryside as its army withdrew to the Hindenburg Line in 1917.

resistance was put up by garrisons at the southern end of the village, on the eastern raiway embankment and at Malassise Farm. The artillery was called into action for the first time that day and after a barrage crashed down on the railway, and at a cost of only one killed and nine wounded, the 6/Gloucester rushed forward and ejected the defenders. By 7.30am the farm had also fallen to the South Midlanders. The brigade extended a little further to the east and dug in on the forward slopes, clear of the burnt and wrecked cottages. The enemy was still in possession of Lempire and Ronssoy, and although he had been chased from Epéhy, the British position was by no means a sinecure. On 5 April 145 Brigade pushed on and, after some ferocious fighting, took the two villages.

As the British line was pushed down Catelet Valley and along the spurs which ran in the direction of the St Quentin Canal, the British position improved still further. Communication trenches wound their laborious way forward, connecting the increasingly well-fortified village with the front line positions. Concrete observation posts were erected and defended areas within the village specified and constructed. The village was often shelled and drenched with gas, but the railway embankments and the slopes to its west provided reasonable cover and protection for troops on rest. It did also have its quieter moments. One officer of the 35th Division recalled that during some periods the enemy remained sufficiently passive for mounted officers to ride most of the way to the front line and complete the remainder of their journey on foot across the open. The village did come under sustained fire during the German counter-attack of 30 November, but as the main enemy thrust was just to the north, its tenure was not immediately in jeopardy. The 55th Division was compelled to give ground along the spurs and valley with the result

March 1918
(See maps
on pages 29
and 32)

that, when the Cambrai battle was over, in places the German outposts were a good 2,000m in advance of where they had been during the summer. The winter snows and frosts handicapped the work of the troops in their attempts to strengthen the village's defences, but when these were tested, they and the troops which manned them played a significant role in holding up the German advance. The dominating position of Peiziere and Epéhy was to be a major objective of the Germans on 21 March 1918. The villages were defended by two battalions of the Leicestershire Regiment, with another in close support to the rear. During the onslaught, these three battalions put up one of the stoutest and longest defences of any in Fifth Army.

The Leicestershire Brigade of the 21st Division moved into the area in December and was immediately put to work. The weather was hardly conducive to easy digging or good trench maintenance, nevertheless large parties were frequently sent to work under the supervision of the divisional RE or Pioneers. Other groups were occasionally dispatched to work on the aerodromes at Nurlu and Cartigny or on the construction of a reserve (Green) line near Moislains. During March, not only did the weather begin to change, but so too did the enemy's attitude. He was seen more frequently in No Man's Land and consistently failed to respond to British shelling. It was clear that he was not prepared to risk having battery locations discovered by sound-ranging or flash-spotting. Enemy prisoners talked of a big attack in preparation and by 17 March, as a consequence of the continuing 'abnormal..[and]...extraordinary inactivity'[1] of the German artillery, the Leicestershire Brigade slightly rearranged its defensive deployment. This involved the withdrawal of Battalion HQ and an additional company of the support unit to Saulcourt. This move almost coincided with a raid by the 6/Leicester on Lark Spur, which resulted in the capture of one man, and a raid by the Germans on a post held by the 7/Leicester, in which Lieutenant Dickinson was killed. The Leicesters were convinced that a major attack was imminent. For the moment, all they could do was wait.

On 21 March companies of the 7/Leicester garrisoned five

German troops surge across No Man's Land in March 1918.

defended localities in the villages; another was ear-marked as the counter-attack company and remained near Battalion HQ at the western end of Peiziere. The 8/Leicester manned the centre and southern portions of Epéhy and the posts to its east. The wire protecting the Forward Zone was considered to be adequate and there were two tanks skulking in reserve near Battalion HQ of the 7th should their services be required.

The German gunners had the several posts, known assembly positions and HQ dugouts neatly registered. When the bombardment crashed down, the 6/Leicester moved off to its battle station through some very accurate shelling. The troops in the brigade's other two battalions took cover. Cumbersome and exhausting gas respirators were worn for at least three hours by troops in all positions. The front line garrisons of the 8/Leicester had been prudently withdrawn to the support trenches and when, at 9.00am, the German barrage shifted to a standing bombardment of the positions west of Epéhy, troops in the Battle Zone knew the infantry attack was under way. The mist allowed the enemy to cross No Man's Land unobserved and he was into Plane Trench and beyond almost before the defenders had time to send off the SOS. The forward trenches were only thinly held, but their garrisons put up a magnificent defence for most of the day. McPhee Post to the north of Peiziere soon fell, but a counter attack by one company, aided by the two tanks, advanced from McLean Post and expelled the intruders.

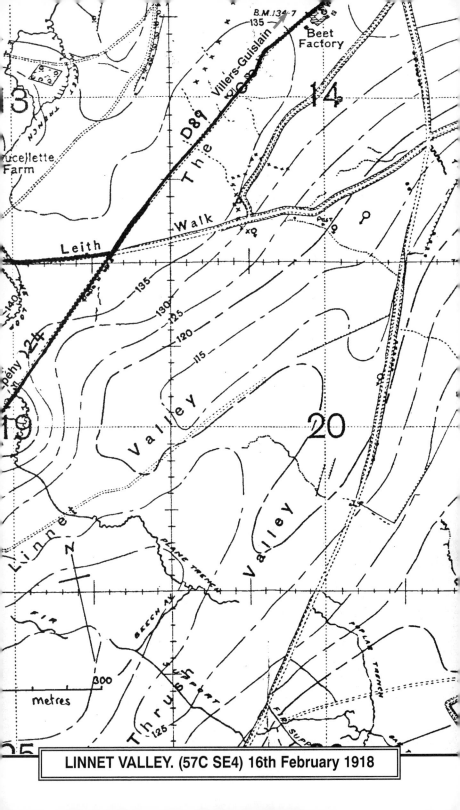

LINNET VALLEY. (57C SE4) 16th February 1918

Fir Support, which lay 600m to the east of the railway and straddled Linnet and Thrush valleys, was attacked by bombers and flammenwerfers. In this sector the mist was beginning to clear and the wire was doing its job. As they struggled to get through the obstacles, the flammenwerfer crews were incinerated by their own weapons. Two or three times Private Hickin walked along the parapet of Fir Support, firing a Lewis from his hip, until he himself was killed. In the afternoon German infantry were seen massing south of Vaucellette Farm (which had fallen around noon) and in Linnet and Thrush Valleys. The mist had by this hour almost entirely dissipated; this allowed the Leicesters and the two tanks to bring down a galling fire upon the enemy troops. The Germans persisted however, and small parties succeeded in penetrating Peiziere from the north. Once again the tanks emerged from their sunken road hideaway and with the assistance of the 7/Leicester's counter-attack company, pushed them out.

Further south, the 8/Leicester had succeeded in repulsing the German attacks on Epéhy. Despite being subjected to fierce Lewis fire and a constant fusillade of rifle grenades, for the time being the enemy seemed content to occupy the Leicesters' original front line. As the mist lifted, enemy troops were seen to be passing through Ronssoy and, before long, trench-mortar shells began to land on Epéhy. Irish troops from the 16th Division scrambled into some of the Leicesters' posts, bringing with them tales of a deep German penetration. In order to conform with a slight readjustment by the 7th Battalion, at about 6.00pm the 8/Leicester was ordered to withdraw to the Battle Zone.

Lewis gun team wearing gas masks in preparation of a German attack.

The Germans did not attack during the night. Having brought up their guns under cover of darkness into the area won from the 16th Division, they began a heavy bombardment early next morning. Infantry attacks again followed the barrage, but were once more driven off. The two stalwart tanks attached to the 7th Battalion were running low on fuel and set off clattering down the road to Saulcourt in search of a fresh supply. Both were knocked out by shell fire on their way and played no further part in the battle. The support battalion, the 6/Leicester, had deployed as a flank guard during the morning. It was assisted by two companies of Royal Engineers; a promised company from the reserve brigade and three Vickers unfortunately failed to materialise. At 9.00am the enemy rushed three posts on the south-eastern edge of the village from the rear and advanced on through the ruins. With the right flank of the 8/Leicester in the air, the Germans threatened to swamp the Battle Zone from the west, east and south. Battalion HQ was moved from Fisher's Keep and a gradual withdrawal executed to maintain contact with the 7/Leicester along the Epéhy-Saulcourt road. A great slaughter of Germans in the valley west of Epéhy took place when the disappearing mist revealed their existence to the flank guard. This action once again delayed the enemy advance, but the damage had been done further south. With the enemy streaming through towards Ste Emilie, at about 11.30am the Leicestershire Brigade was ordered to fight its way back to Longavesnes. The 6th and 8th Battalions slipped away through Saulcourt, while Captain Vanner of the 7th blew two bridges over the railway cutting just north of Peiziere in the hope of delaying the pursuing guns and transport.

The Leicesters had demonstrated what a brigade in the Forward and Battle Zones could achieve. With the front trenches lightly but resolutely held to delay and disorganise, and with the redoubts well stocked with ammunition and protected by wire, enemy attacks were repeatedly broken up. Assisted by a clearing mist, the advantage of good observation, the availability of tanks and some disorganisation caused by the enemy's gas drifting back over his own lines, the troops in the Battle Zone did what had been anticipated. Unfortunately for 110 Brigade, the enemy penetration of the 16th Division's defences to the south and the fall of Vaucellette Farm to the north exposed it to the danger of encirclement. The brigade withdrew in good order and lived to fight another day.

The first division to attempt the recapture of Epéhy in September September 1918 1918 was the 58th. It relieved one of its sister London Divisions and, with 175 Brigade in the van, attacked towards Saulcourt Wood on 7

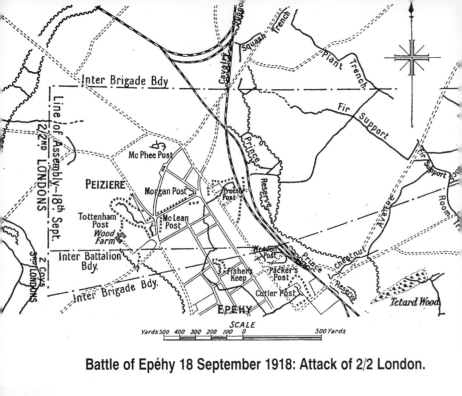

Battle of Epéhy 18 September 1918: Attack of 2/2 London.

September. The brigade came under fire from Epéhy but secured Ste Emilie. The following day, 174 Brigade followed through and assaulted Epéhy and Peiziere. Progress was slow and further hampered by repeated German counter-attacks. Division decided to pause for one full day to allow more artillery preparation and on 10 September, while the 74th Division made an attempt on Ronssoy Wood, 173 Brigade again went for the twin villages. The staff were not sure whether the German resistance was merely a prolonged rearguard action or whether the British had finally come upon the major line of defence. Two battalions of Territorial City Fusiliers were ordered to get through Wood Farm and into Peiziere, while a sister battalion approached from the south-west. Simultaneous with the Fusiliers' assault on Prince Reserve was an attack by the 21st Division on Vaucellette Farm and Chapel Crossing. Zero was 5.15am and there was some initial success. The 2/2 London got through to Prince Reserve while the 3/London passed through Epéhy and reached the railway embankment beyond.

(See map on page 32)

However, the artillery had failed to silence a good number of the enemy scattered in and around the village. As it was already coming under enfilade fire and in danger of envelopment, the 2/2 London, while maintaining a hold on Tottenham Post, withdrew to the west of Peiziere. The task had, in the words of one of the regimental histories, 'proved too much'[2] for a brigade which could muster only some 900 men. Nevertheless, the attack was renewed in the afternoon and an attempt made to secure a line from McPhee Post to Morgan Post. The Londoners employed infiltration tactics, but with little success. The attack was ill-prepared and it was realised that a more substantial effort would have to be made if the enemy was to be ejected from Epéhy. For the next week the Londoners contented themselves with patrolling and consolidation.

The main street of Epéhy as it looked to British troops in September 1918.
IWM Q105456

33

Three soldiers of the 12th Division take a break from their labours outside Epéhy, 18 September 1918. IWM Q11326

A raid on the Rangers, who were holding Tottenham Post on 12 September, was broken up by artillery targeting the enemy's assembly position in Wood Farm.

In order to give the assaulting troops a greater chance of success, Z day was postponed for two days while further artillery preparations were made. The first objective for 173 Brigade was the railway embankment just east of Peiziere; once that was secured, it was to go for Fir Support and

Poplar Trench another 1500m to the east. On its right, 35 Brigade of the 12th Division was to use the 7/Norfolk, 9/Essex and two tanks, assisted by two companies of the 1/1 Cambridgeshire for its attack on Epéhy. The 21st Division on the left was to have another go at the ridge to the north of the village. Once again the 2/2 London led the way, with the 2/24th following behind to mop up. The 3/London had the task of filling the gap between its 2nd Battalion and 35 Brigade to the right. The battalion's tasks were to take Fisher's Keep and to provide garrisons for McPhee, Morgan and Proctor Posts once they had fallen.

Dawn of 18 September was slow to arrive and murky when it did. At 5.30am the British line moved forward and within an hour the 2/2 London was on the railway embankment. The advance continued to Fir Trench and the Germans in Morgan and McLean Posts either surrendered or fled. 62nd Brigade cleared the ridge to the north and, by mid-day, only Fisher's Keep and Proctor Post were still holding out. The Norfolks and Essex took the southern end of Epéhy, and a combined attack by the 3/London and the 1/1 Cambridgeshire eventually overcame Fisher's Keep. The remaining Germans in the village retreated to the east, and by 8.15pm the Berkshires had secured the trenches lying between Tetard Wood and Chestnut Avenue. An

German prisoners and their escort march over the railway track in Epéhy, and into captivity. 18 September 1918. IWM Q11335

attack on Poplar Trench at 9.00pm by the 2/2 London failed, but the battalion did establish three posts immediately to its front. At 11.00am the following morning, the Londoners resumed the offensive. After a strenuous eight hours of bombing they had cleared the length of Poplar Trench and were in touch with 37 Brigade in Room Trench on their right.

Epéhy and Peiziere were cleared of the enemy and the British were in approximately the same positions as they had been at the beginning of April of the previous year. There remained, however, plenty of hard fighting to be done on the spurs running down to the canal before the 58th, 18th and 12th Divisions could look upon the Hindenburg Line.

Notes

1. War Diary of 8/Leicester. WO.95.2165
2. W.Grey, *The 2nd City of London Regiment (RF) in the Great War,* p.373

Epéhy today

This substantial village consists of a sprawling and untidy main street, with an equally ugly estate of poor housing known as *la Cité Blanche*. A new development of family housing (which includes a *Rue des Anglais*), relieves the overall unfortunate aspect of the village.

Few wartime relics remain. The two principal exceptions are the observation posts near Cullen and Morgan Posts. The railway station is largely derelict but sugar trains do run through from Ste Emilie. One of the grander buildings is an old people's home on the main street. There is a narrow gravel path leading down from the road which runs parallel to and 200m west of the main road. Either side of the path is the site of Fisher's Keep. Scores of British screw pickets support the fence along the route of the path.

The adjoining village of Peiziere is a refreshing contrast. It retains a charm with pleasant housing and cultivated gardens. Tottenham Post now lies under a smart house on a minor road east of Wood Farm. The crossroads to the south of this house marks the site of McLean Post. 600m down the left turn is a small copse and bank. This was the Battalion HQ of the 7/Leicester on 21 March. The lane curls round past the copse and divides. The left fork was probably the hideaway of the two tanks which gave such welcome support to the Leicesters.

The communal cemetery lies to the south-east of the village, just west of the railway. Epéhy Wood Farm Cemetery is to the west of the village on the Saulcourt road.

Tour of Epéhy
(Tour Map 1)
5kms, 3miles. 1.25 hours

Park at the church towards the southern end of the village. Take the small road opposite (C5) – at the CWGC sign towards Pigeon Ravine Cemetery. Visit the civilian cemetery and return past the observation post at Cullen Post. **(1)** This is in a garden 30m north of the C5. Take the road past the post and continue heading north. It passes the

The British observation tower at Cullen Post.

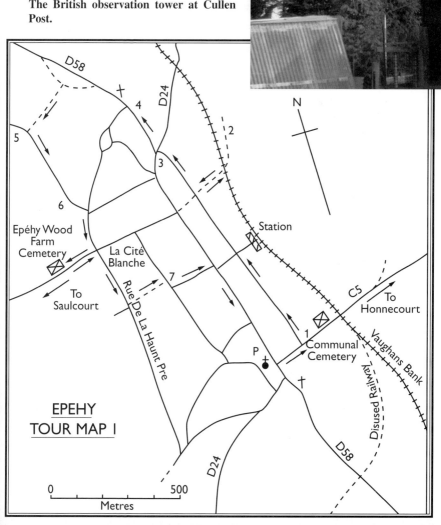

This observation tower at Morgan Post, at the northern end of the village, was defended by the 7/Leicester on 21 March 1918.

largely derelict station. Beyond the station there are good views down Thrush and Linnet Valleys. **(2)** These are much the same views as those obtained from the concrete observation post at Morgan's Post. This is found in the farm 50m before the cobbled road joins the D24. **(3)**

At the road go almost straight over and join the D58 towards Heudicourt. The farm on the right just after the junction marks the site of McPhee Post. **(4)** 300m after the crucifix, the route of the old road can be seen on the left. Take the grass path which joins the old road and follow it to the copse lining a small lane coming from Epéhy. This is the site of the 7/Leicester HQ. **(5)**

Turn left towards Epéhy, passing the farmhouse which marks the site of Tottenham Post at the end of the lane. **(6)** Bear right and then turn right at the crossroads to walk down the Saulcourt road to Epéhy Wood Farm Cemetery. Retrace your route to the crossroads. Turn right down the *Rue de l'Haut Pre*. After 230m take the path on the left which goes between two fields. The eastern end of this path marks the site of Fisher's Keep. **(7)** Turn right and left. This brings you back to the village's central road. Turn right to return to your car.

Linnet and Thrush Valleys, with Vaucellette Farm on the left and Villers-Guislain on the right. This is almost the view British observers would have had from Morgan Post.

Chapter Two

CHAPEL CROSSING

In the appalling weather of early 1917, one New Army and one regular division gradually pushed their way towards the large village of Gouzeaucourt. The 8th Division approached the ruins, which lay on the

**April
1917**

The gently rolling land to the west of Vaucellette Farm. Gauche Wood is in the far distance and the undistinguished mound of Chapel Hill, centre left. The sporadic line of trees from the right edge lead up to Chapel Crossing.

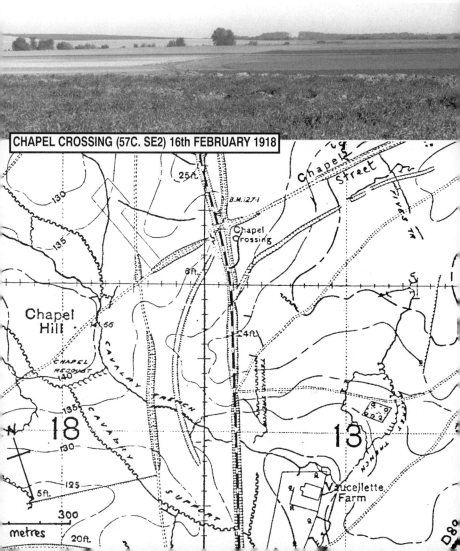

(See map
page 40)

top of a significant spur, from the south and west. During the night of
1-2 April, the 1/Worcester occupied a line facing approximately east,
to the west of the railway line north of Peiziere. The following night, in
conditions which alternated from penetrating sleet to all enveloping
snow, the battalion pushed on over the slight rise on its front and seized
Vaucellette Farm. The following 24 hours were spent in skirmishing
between the farm and Chapel Crossing, some 400m to the north.
However, as

> *'the weather on the heights was too wild and the whole
> situation too vague for any serious fighting',*[1]

**Two German guns and their horses near Villers-Guislain, caught and
destroyed by British artillery.**

the battalion sustained only three wounded.

There were still some standing buildings at Vaucellette Farm when the site was occupied by units of the 8th Division. These included a large concrete shelter which had been used as a billet by the crew of a rail-mounted gun. The weapon had been withdrawn, but the cutting through which the track passed provided excellent protection for the new occupants of the farm.

Gouzeaucourt fell to 24 Brigade on 12 April; two days later 23 Brigade, having cleared Gauche Wood, pressed on to Villers-Guislain. Dense wire, machine-gun fire and heavy snow prevented the 2/Devon from penetrating the village, but after a few days of concentrated shelling, the wire was cut sufficiently to allow the 2/West Yorks to fight their way through and complete the capture. For the West Yorkshires, it had been a protracted and miserable affair. Struggling through sleet and snow a patrol of the battalion had entered the beet factory south-west of Villers-Guislain on 12 April, capturing three equally cold Germans. The enemy subsequently sent about 150 men to surround the new British position and following a fierce exchange of fire, the West Yorkshires withdrew.

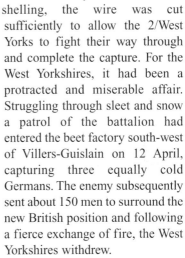

At dusk the same day the battalion launched a larger attack on the beet factory and the crest beyond while the 2/Scottish Rifles went for Gauche Wood. The troops formed up in the sunken lane leading to Vaucellette Farm and with the help of a Stokes bombardment, once again entered the rapidly disintegrating beet factory. The Germans withdrew and contented themselves with putting a variety of shells onto the buildings all the following day. A very uncomfortable battalion was relieved by the 2/Middlesex on 14 April and trudged back to Guyencourt. The weather remained awful and the West Yorkshires' scheduled attack on Villers-Guislain for 4.00pm on 17th was mercifully postponed. However, it could not be delayed indefinitely and at 11.30pm, following a hot meal at Guyencourt, the battalion began the four mile trek towards its jumping off point 600 metres south-west of the village. At 3.15am on 18 April, with the men in position on the tapes, a ration of rum was swallowed and the men handed in their greatcoats. The covering barrage began at 4.25am and the troops climbed and slithered from their slimy pits and shell holes to pass through the 2/Middlesex. Covering the ground between the tapes and the village in about 20 minutes, the four companies entered the village. The defenders put up little resistance and their defensive barrage landed on the positions now empty of Yorkshiremen. By 6.00am all objectives had been gained and the two supporting battalions had come up on the flanks.

By the end of April, Vaucellette Farm, Chapel Crossing and Gauche Wood were approximately 5000m behind the front British positions. They were quickly utilised by battalions in brigade reserve and, during the summer months, hutted camps were built to their rear. Light railways were laid and shelters constructed along the courses of both the line to Cambrai and the track which ran west towards Fins. This latter line, which branched off the Chapel Crossing track just north of

Two dead British soldiers lie near Vaucellette Farm. This German photo shows them stripped of their boots. IWM

Vaucellette Farm today. It is still owned by the same family who occupied the site in 1914.

Peiziere, was relaid with broad gauge steel as far as Heudicourt. Activity along the front lines to the east rarely ceased but, apart from the habitual spell of daily shelling, the ridge along which the three features sat was often quiet. The situation changed dramatically on the morning of 30 November 1917.

In this sector the German counter-strike against the Cambrai **November** offensive fell upon the extremely under-strength 55th Division. The **1917** West Lancashire Territorials held a front of 13,000m, not as continuous trenches but as a series of largely unconnected posts. The divisional boundary with the 12th Division to the north was held by the 5/South Lancs. This unfortunate battalion had a front of scattered posts stretching for over 2000m. Its only reserve in the area through which the main German thrust was to come was constituted by two platoons of the 5/King's Own. During the evening of 29 November Battalion HQ sent this uncompromising message to its four companies:

'In the event of attack, you will hold the line at all costs. There is to be no retirement to any second line'.

Once the left company in the valley between Villers-Guislain and Gonnelieu had been eliminated, the enemy entered Villers-Guislain from the north-east. Divisional and corps artillery were surprised by the sudden appearance of German infantry emerging from the mist, but firing over open sights and with instantaneous fuses, the guns roared until their detachments were overwhelmed. Some crews managed to escape but in Villers-Guislain, VII and III Corps lost a combined total of 58 guns.

Another escapee was Brigadier-General Berkeley Vincent, GOC 33 Brigade. He just managed to escape from his HQ dugout in Villers-Guislain before it was surrounded by enemy troops. With about 100 assorted men he retired, via Gauche Wood and the railway embankment behind, to Révelon Ridge and there took command of two reserve battalions of the 12th Division, a company of the 5/Northants (Pioneers) and three machine guns. As more troops fell back, a line of

(See map
page 29) Gauche Wood as seen from the beet factory. After the German counter-
attack during the Battle of Cambrai, the British front line was only yards
in front of the wood's dismembered trees.

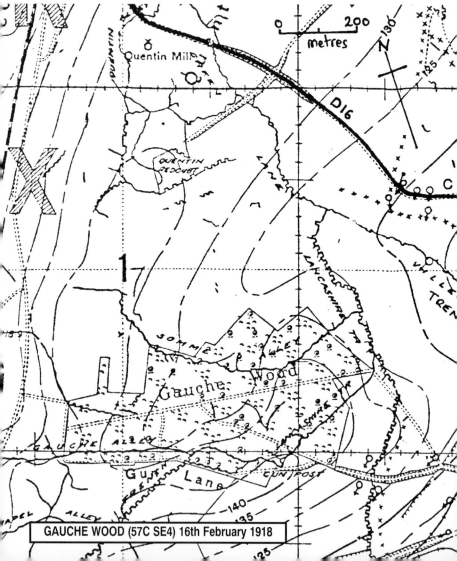

GAUCHE WOOD (57C SE4) 16th February 1918

sorts was established along Révelon Ridge, northwards towards Gouzeaucourt. The defenders were known as Vincent's Force and comprised Northumberland Hussars, 12th Division details, cyclists, the band of the Royal Dragoons and some Monmouth Pioneers. To the right front of this force were elements of the 55th Division.

On the evening of 28 November, men of the 1/4 Loyal North Lancashire were issued with an extra 50 rounds and told to stand by. Nothing came of that particular alert, so the battalion was marched back to Vaucellette Camp. At 9.00am on 30 November, hordes of British infantry were seen to be pouring back towards Heudicourt and reports arrived that the artillery was abandoning its guns in Villers-Guislain. Battalion HQ under the RSM was sent forward to establish a line running north-east of the farm. Immediately the Loyals appeared in the open, they came under fire from machine guns in Villers-Guislain and Chapel Crossing. Rapidly digging in, the battalion managed to stem the German tide. The enemy later settled on a line stretching 1400m from the beet factory to Chapel Crossing. Both flanks of the Loyals were reported to be in the air but so critical and unclear had the general situation become around Gauche Wood, Gouzeaucourt and Villers-Guislain that the battalion was ordered to advance in open order and clear the enemy from Villers Hill. Led by Colonel Hindle and firing Lewis guns and rifles as they went, the troops advanced through a hail of bullets. When the centre of their line was only about 200m from the crest and with their ammunition almost exhausted, the Loyals were confronted by enemy reinforcements swarming over the hill. At this decisive moment Colonel Hindle was killed; the survivors withdrew across the valley and up the slope towards Vaucellette Farm. Resupplied with ammunition by stretcher bearers, the battalion dug in on the eastern side of the farm. An advance post was established by Major Crump (who appeared on the scene to undertake a reconnaissance on behalf of 166 Brigade), comprising one Vickers and a crew drawn from several regiments. This gun did great execution on waves of enemy infantry advancing up Leith Walk.

Just after mid-day a composite battalion of the 12th Division moved up to join the 6/Queen's, who had set off earlier. Both battalions succeeded in making contact with the Loyals at the farm. Having acquired another Vickers, Major Crump kept one gun covering the approaches up Linnet Valley and sent the other to the farm. A new trench was dug south of the farm with tools brought forward by the Loyals' Battalion Mobile Reserve of SAA. This trench was connected to the one already manned to the east of the farm and was wired during the hours of darkness. As night fell, some dismounted Northumberland Hussars began digging a support trench to the rear of the farm and, in the early hours of 1 December, the Loyals handed over their trench to the composite battalion and went into reserve in dugouts in the railway embankment. Fighting strength had been reduced to 15 officers and 351 other ranks, but the action had won the battalion three MCs, two DCMs and 18 MMs.

Plans to counter-attack the German onslaught were being hurriedly made and what preparations were possible were set in train. An attack against Chapel Crossing, Gauche Wood and the beet factory was to be a joint effort by mounted and dismounted cavalry, infantry and tanks. There was some artillery support, but in the event it proved to be patchy and largely ineffective.

Plans were, of necessity, rather haphazard. The cavalry knew little of the infantry's dispositions and even less of the availability of tanks. The steel monsters were dangerously low on fuel and in desperate need of servicing. Despite the lack of clear intelligence and a significant shortage of all calibres of artillery, the attack was scheduled for a few minutes before 7.00am. The 36th Jacob's Horse and Jodhpur Lancers formed up dismounted on the Villers-Guislain–Peiziere road about 600m south of Vaucellette Farm. As they moved forward, assisted by a section of the 12th MG Squadron, the tired defenders of the farm were apparently 'heartened by the sight'[2] of the ferocious-looking sowars. The advance of the cavalry was halted soon after they cleared the shoulder of ground on which the farm stands and came in sight of the Germans covering Chapel Crossing. A withering fire from enemy troops in a line of shell hole stretching across to the beet factory forced the Jacob's and Lancers to seek cover.

The Inniskilling Dragoons, supplemented by a section of 11th MG Squadron and a field troop of RE, also attempted the same route. They charged down the road and across the adjacent open fields, gaining considerably more ground than the Jacob's, but were also stopped by fire coming from the occupied shell holes near to the beet factory. The survivors were soon surrounded and captured. Another attempt to reach the beet factory was made in the afternoon by other units of the Lucknow Brigade, but this too ended in bloody failure.

Further north, 1 Guards Brigade had made a brilliant charge up the slope towards Gauche Wood. Initially unaccompanied by tanks which turned up ten minutes after zero, the 2/Grenadiers stormed up the hill towards the wood from the north. The German defenders were surprised by the speed of the advance and, although pressing home at least two counter-attacks, failed to eject the Guards from the wood. The 18/Lancers, and several tanks which had managed to regain their bearings, came up to support the Grenadiers and secure the wood. Other dismounted cavalry, including Hodson's Horse who lost two of its squadron commanders, arrived soon after and the work of consolidation began. Spurred on by this success, dismounted Canadians moved up. Chapel Crossing was retaken and a line extended to link with the defenders of the farm to the east of the railway. To the north of Gauche Wood, the 3/Coldstream Guards, led by four tanks, had taken their objective of Quentin Ridge with little difficulty and immediately established two machine guns between the wood and the Gouzeaucourt – Villers-Guislain road which began to pour fire into the German positions in Gonnelieu.

The German counter-offensive had caused major problems for the

A wave of German assault troops move across No Man's Land

British, but with the fall of darkness on 1 December the worst was over. The farm, the crossing and Gauche Wood were to remain in British hands for nearly another four months. The 21st Division relieved the remnants of the cavalry, the 12th and the 55th Divisions shortly after the German counter-attack was halted. One of the earliest tasks was to bury the large numbers of frozen corpses that lay strewn around the farm and its environs. The 9th Division, with the South African Brigade attached to it, took over responsibility for the defence of Gauche Wood. The enemy line lay at the foot of the slope running down from the wood, with the ruins of Villers-Guislain remaining in German hands. Chapel Crossing once again became a British possession and the low crest to its west was developed into one of the redoubts designed to break up any future German attacks. Gauche Wood and the farm also received a great deal of attention during the winter months and, like Chapel Hill, were consolidated into redoubts. The difficulties of winter and of the British manpower shortages necessitated a comparatively passive routine of trench holding. Patrols did, of course, crawl across No Man's Land and occasionally raided enemy listening and advanced posts. In addition to the inevitable challenges from the elements, digging, wiring and efforts to gain intelligence on movements behind enemy lines remained the priorities for British troops. As evidence of a major German offensive grew, patrols became more frequent. Defence schemes were finalised and practised, and the storm awaited.

March 1918 The German dam burst upon the defenders of the three features on the misty morning of 21 March. Vaucellette Farm was garrisoned by troops of the 12/13 Northumberland Fusiliers. It was the 21st Division's right battalion of the left brigade. A week before the German attack, the battalion had conducted a large raid with 100 men under the command of Lieutenant Hutchinson. It netted no prisoners and, during the four days preceding the offensive's opening, the enemy was described as being 'unusually quiet'.[3] Like the twin villages of Epéhy and Peiziere, the farm, Chapel Hill and Gauche Wood were really in the Forward rather than the Battle Zone. The farm was only about 500 yards behind the front posts. These were soon overrun and the redoubt itself fell about noon. As few survivors emerged from its broken ruins to write an account of its fall, little is known of the precise events surrounding its capture. Battalion HQ, which was sited in the railway embankment south of the farm, also fell quickly. Lieutenant-Colonel R.Howlett was away on leave, but the temporary CO and four other senior officers were killed or captured when the enemy emerged from the mist and entered their dugout.

The fortunes of the brigade's left battalion, the 1/Lincolnshire, were a little better than those of the Fusiliers. 62 Brigade was rather unusual as it contained two regular battalions of the same regiment. The 2/Lincolnshire had undertaken a raid on Beet Trench one week after the Northumberlands had carried out theirs a little to the south. The Lincolns brought back five prisoners and were relieved by their sister battalion the same night. According to the brigade defence scheme, the 1/Lincolnshire had one company holding Birdwood Copse, one in the trenches to the south of Chapel Hill, one in Chapel Street and the fourth in reserve on Chapel Hill. If the front positions were overrun, survivors were supposed to retire upon the redoubt. A company of the support battalion (2/Lincolnshire) and two tanks stationed in the railway embankment, would be available as counter-attack troops.

Birdwood Copse was lost in the opening minutes of the attack. Because the fall of the farm exposed its flank, what was left of the copse's garrison fell back to Chapel Hill. Bitter fighting for the redoubt continued for some hours. One company of the 2/Lincolnshire went forward as planned to help in its defence, and formed a defensive flank running from the redoubt to Genin Well Copse. Some South African Scottish arrived to swell the number of defenders but, with the fall of Vaucellette Farm to the south and Gauche Wood to the north, the Lincolns and South Africans were ordered to relinquish their hold on the hill. At about 4.00pm they withdrew to the Green Line, which in places was more of a concept than a reality, and dug in. The 11/Royal Scots came up to help the South Africans defend a trench dug by the 9/Seaforths between the hill and Railton; the Germans were through in such numbers that the defenders were soon withdrawn to Haute Allaines and Gurlu Wood. A counter-attack by the 15/DLI at 8.00pm retook a strong point just to the west of the farm, but could make no further progress.

The South African Brigade fought hard for Gauche Wood and its task was made yet more difficult by the receipt of several confusing reports. The wood was held by one company of the 2nd Regiment. It manned three posts within the wood itself and another in the open ground just to the south-west. The Germans launched a frontal attack on Captain Green's company from the east and used infiltration tactics to get into the wood from its northern face. Two posts were almost immediately overrun, the survivors joining the garrison of the third. Weight of numbers soon forced them from their trenches and positions among the shattered tree stumps. They dug in to the west of the wood

Wounded British and German troops moving to the rear. The man with the leg wound belongs to a pioneer battalion.

and, with their comrades in the post in the open ground, maintained a withering fire on the enemy as he attempted to debouch. For their continued efforts to throw their men against the South African positions, German commanders were later described as being 'prodigal of life'.[4] The carnage was made worse when British artillery brought down a bombardment on the newly won positions within the wood. However, weight of numbers again told, and the South Africans began a fighting retreat towards Gouzeaucourt and Révelon Ridge.

Casualties on both sides had been heavy. Fresh German troops poured through the valley behind Chapel Hill and the farm, passing over the bodies of their comrades killed by concentrated fire from Epéhy and the hill. Weary, often dispirited British soldiers, with tales of widespread collapse on several sectors and the sight of artillery batteries limbering up and galloping to the west, added to the air of despondency and confusion. The German surge continued and Fifth Army soon lost sight of its former defended localities. It plodded and fought its way back across the land where Fourth Army had pursued the retreating Germans 12 months earlier.

The British retreat was so rapid that many camps and dumps were left intact and, much to the consternation of their commanders, the contents were hugely enjoyed by the enemy soldiers. The tide of battle flowed back across the old Somme battlefields, and the farm, Chapel Hill and Gauche Wood became again reserve and rest areas for the German army. Troops in the area, labour companies, prisoners of war and civilians rebuilt the partly damaged defences of the Hindenburg Line. They laid yet more fields of wire in Linnet, Thrush and the other so quaintly named valleys and repositioned the former British trenches to provide outpost and advanced positions along the ridges and forward slopes. When the BEF again appeared on the rolling plain and approached the three features, the defences were once more formidable.

In September 1918, V Corps approached the the farm, crossing and wood from the south and west. The scheme was to recapture Chapel Hill as a first objective and then to extend east to take both the crossing and the farm. The recapture of the wood was part of the third objective. By keeping largely to the high ground, the villages of Gouzeaucourt and Villers-Guislain could be overlooked, and the former eventually surrounded.

September 1918

By an uncanny occurrence of coincidence, the 21st Division, which had lost two of the features in March, was one of the two divisions entrusted with their recapture. The 17th and 38th Divisions, with the 33rd in reserve, were the other elements of V Corps. No tanks were available to assist the attacks, so the infantry relied upon a creeping barrage, an enormous amount of smoke and low-flying aircraft. The two Lincolnshire battalions and the 12/13 NF swept forward to take the farm and the railway crossing, but the 6/Leicester on the right was held up because the 58th Division was making slow progress through the Leicesters' old stomping ground of Peiziere. The 7/Border, in the centre of the 17th Division's attack, fought hard to get into Gauche Wood. Once a resilient machine-gun nest constructed from four derelict British tanks had been finally subdued by 6-inch trench-mortar fire, the wood was cleared. C Company bombed the enemy from his trenches and dug in just to the east of the wood. From their new positions, British troops once again had observation over Villers-Guislain. The 7/Lincolnshire reached the wood's northern edge and beat off several counter-attacks later in the day. During a night attack the 6/Dorset pressed on to take the former British stronghold of

Quentin redoubt; at the same time the 10/West Yorkshire took a trench on its southern edge. The high ground dominating Gouzeaucourt and Villers-Guislain was once again in British hands. If they happened to wander above the mass graves of their comrades buried by the Germans since the spring offensive, any March survivors in the Lincolnshire and Northumberlands could perhaps reflect on having settled an old score.

In the early hours of 29 September two brigades of the 33rd Division attacked Villers-Guislain from the south.[5] Confused by mist, poor light and intense enemy resistance, 98 and 100 Brigades were bloodily repulsed. One of the three tanks which started and some infantry of 98 Brigade did get into the eastern end of the village but a German counter-attack soon cleared most of them out. More enemy troops were seen to be filtering into the north of the village and pressing around the flanks. To avoid encirclement, the survivors of the two battalions withdrew to their own start line. Shelling continued for most of the day but at about 8.00am on 30 September, the enemy were discovered to have evacuated the village. Patrols pushed into the ruins and dug in on the crest beyond.

Notes

1. H.Stacke, *The Worcestershire Regiment in the Great War,* p.248
2. *Official History 1917, The Battle of Cambrai,* p.232
3. War Diary of 12/13 Northumberland Fusiliers, 14 March 1918. WO.95.2155
4. J.Ewing, *The History of the 9th(Scottish) Division 1914-18,* p.262
5. See 'East of Epéhy' for an account of the attack by the 2/Worcester.

The Chapel Crossing area today

(See map pages 6 - 7)

Sitting on top of a spur, Vaucellette Farm, with its white-roofed outbuildings and surrounding trees, is visible from all directions. Similarly, Gauche Wood is easily identified as it is the only wood of any size in the district. Apart from the occasional tractor and the odd car avoiding the main road between Villers-Guislain and Gouzeaucourt, the elderly bridge over Chapel Crossing is rarely used. Chapel Street leads directly to the crossing from Villers-Guislain. Once over the railway, the tarmac follows the railway cutting north until the ground falls away sufficiently to allow vehicles to cross the line. It then continues to join the D16 near a quarry which the 2/RB and other units used as a cemetery from April 1917. **(1)**

Chapel Hill is difficult to identify other than as a mound only marginally higher than its surroundings. To its right front is Birdwood Copse and Vaucellette Farm. The farm is private property and can properly only be observed from the bottom of its access road. A memorial to the 1/4 LNL was apparently erected at the farm after the war. However, the current owner, whose grandfather rebuilt the farm in the 1920s, does not know of its existence. The former German shelter is now only a lump of concrete, largely buried within a bed of nettles. It is not worth invading the farmer's privacy to view. There are many other more extensive and easily observable shelters within the area.

Gauche Wood has recently been opened up for public access. The central path can be walked along its entire length. 200m from the eastern end is the remains of what might have been a British elephant shelter. Gauche Alley is clearly identified just inside the southern edge at the western end and part of Lancashire Trench can be followed inside its south-eastern face. The soil of the wood remains punctured by numerous shell holes and shallow trench lines. The site of Quentin mill is now occupied by kennels **(2)** and should be approached with care. Quentin redoubt **(3)** can be reached by a lane (which begins as tarmac but becomes grass within 100m), 800m east of the railway on the D16. Villers-Guislain communal cemetery, with its plot of 50 British graves, lies 600m west of the village.

All that remains of the once substantial German block house at Vaucellette Farm. Usually buried beneath nettles and undergrowth, and on private land, there is little to see.

Tour of Chapel Hill and its surrounds
(Tour Map 2)
14kms, 8.75miles. 3.5 hours

Park at Villers-Guislain *Mairie* and walk along the D16 towards Gouzeaucourt. Visit the communal cemetery with the British plot at the far end. Continue along the D16 and turn left onto a gravel track 800m after the cemetery. As you walk towards Gauche Wood, the site of Quentin Redoubt **(3)** is on the hill to your right. When the gravel

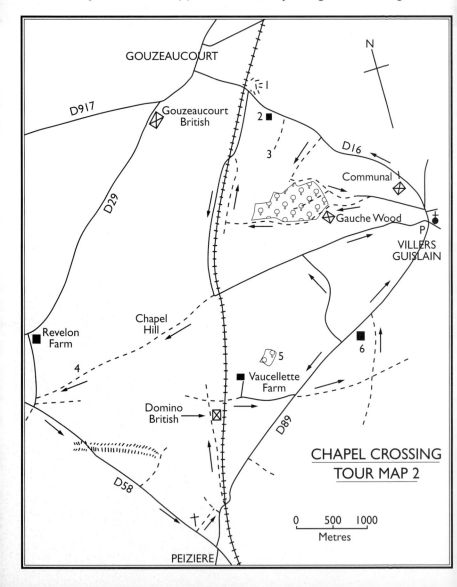

GOUZEAUCOURT

D917

Gouzeaucourt
British

D29

1

2

3

D16

Communal

Gauche Wood

P

VILLERS
GUISLAIN

N

Chapel
Hill

Revelon
Farm

4

5

6

Vaucellette
Farm

Domino
British

D89

D58

PEIZIERE

CHAPEL CROSSING
TOUR MAP 2

0   500   1000
Metres

The railway embankment running between Epéhy and Heudicourt. A culvert on the right tunnels through the bank and there are several depressions which indicate the numerous dugouts which once housed battalion HQs and counter-attack companies before 21 March.

ends, turn 90 degrees left and walk up the face of the wood. Near the top of the hill a track leads into the wood. The remains of the (possibly) British elephant shelter is 200m inside the wood on your left.

Continue on the track, which has now become gravel, as if dropping down into Villers-Guislain. After 300m take the lane to the sharp right which usually has a CWGC sign at the junction. Climb up the lane to Gauche Wood Cemetery.

From the cemetery turn left and walk through 200m of the wood. You emerge on its southern face. The line of Gauche Alley can be discerned in the final section of the wood. Follow the headland for 150m down to a more convincing track and turn right. This runs parallel to the railway and after 500m pick up another track and cross the railway. The road climbs above the railway cutting and turns left at Chapel Crossing.

Chapel Hill is 600m to the west of Chapel Crossing. The track is normally passable and continues on down past the site of Genin Well Copses No.2, **(4)** now just a few trees, and on to Railton.

This dilapidated and forlorn building stands on the site of the beet factory south of Villers-Guislain. It is used for several nefarious purposes, most notably, dumping.

Gauche Wood Cemetery squats comfortably on the ridge to the east of the wood. In the trees to the right, behind some abandoned beehives, are the easily identifiable remains of Lancashire Trench.

Révelon Farm and Ridge are above you on your right.

The old track to Vaucellette Farm from Railton disappears after 1400m so join the D58 and walk towards Epéhy. The road crosses the old railway after 700m. The embankment on your left was used by battalion HQ and counter-attack companies. Just before Epéhy, take the grass path after the crucifix, turn right when it joins the track of the old railway and left onto the D89. Immediately before the level crossing is the CWGC sign to Domino Cemetery. Follow it and visit the cemetery. Continue up to a junction of tracks and turn right to cross the railway. This track passes the access road into Vaucellette Farm. Cavalry Support Trench crossed the land 50m east of the railway.

Continue on until the D89 is reached. Here there are several options: 1) turn left and walk up the road, past the ruined beet factory and into Villers-Guislain. 2) turn left and left again onto a tarmac road before the beet factory. **(6)** This drops down past Birdwood Copse **(5)** and joins Chapel Street on the opposite side of the valley. Follow this down into Villers-Guislain. 3) Go straight across the D89 and join Leith Walk. This track, which in summer is heavily protected by nettles, drops into Linnet Valley. Turn left at a junction of tracks and climb up to rejoin the D89 by Villers-Guislain water tower.

Chapter Three

GONNELIEU

Ignored by the old Roman road connecting Péronne with Cambrai by several score metres to the north, Gonnelieu stands in happy semi-isolation. It is an unremarkable village, typical in size and characteristic of many in the area. It probably remained unseen or unnoticed by the retreating BEF in August 1914 and would have retained its insignificance in British eyes until the German retreat of

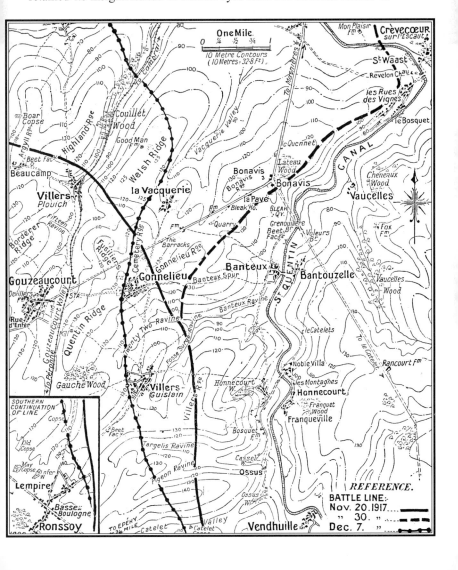

March 1917. Once the enemy had occupied his new positions, the ridge on which the village sits acquired a new importance. If it could be taken it would provide a useful observation platform for British forces. The ground falls away sharply to north and south and drops even more steeply towards the canal at Banteux. Having sited their outpost line on the eastern crest of the ridge, the Germans did not of course intend that the pursuing forces should secure any easy advantage.

Having taken Gouzeaucourt on the 12th and Villers-Guislain on 14 April, the 8th Division prepared to continue the advance and attack Gonnelieu and its ridge. The position was all the more important for it gave the Germans good observation of the other two recently captured villages. Although aerial reconnaissance had shown that the Hindenburg Line lay east of the village, it was by no means certain that the enemy would not stand and fight in this, the last collection of buildings west of his new line of resistance. Parts of the line and beyond could already be seen by units of 23 Brigade; on the night of 20 April several farms and villages behind the position were reported to be burning.

Wire cutting had been commenced by the divisional artillery on the previous day and it continued on through the 20th in preparation for an attack by 25 Brigade. The assault was to be a combined effort. The 2/Lincoln and 2/RB would go for the village while 119 Brigade of the 40th Division would attack the spur, later christened Fusilier Ridge, north of the main Cambrai road. A creeping barrage supplemented by a standing bombardment of artillery and machine guns heralded the infantry advance which began at 4.20am. Advance patrols of the Lincolnshire cut gaps through the wire without a shot being fired but, as they called up their support companies, heavy rifle fire erupted. On their left the Battle Platoon Patrol of the 2/RB advanced in four-strong sections between the Cambrai road and the smaller road between Gouzeaucourt and Gonnelieu, in touch with both the 19/RWF and the Lincolns. Two companies were to support the advanced patrols and, when they saw four Very lights fired by the Lincolns to confirm they had taken the village, they would enter it from the north. The lights were subsequently observed but, when the RB advanced, it came under sustained fire from the chateau and several other buildings. The Battle Platoon Patrol was ordered to hold on in its positions and to get on into the village if possible while the companies worked around the flank. They were assisted by an attack undertaken by the 19/RWF on one of the strong points to the north-west of the village which was also hampering the RB's advance. Once the Fusiliers had silenced that post, they then gave covering fire to the 'black buttons' as they entered the village. After some fighting amongst the houses and orchards the RB joined up with the Lincolns at the east end of the main street. The eventual haul amounted to 88 German prisoners and 51 machine guns while the RB lost 13 dead and 49 wounded in the attack. The success of the operation was

> 'due to the initiative and courage of the Battle Platoon Patrol which held on to all ground gained under heavy fire and the quickness with which the attacking companies outflanked the enemy positions'.[1]

This last village before the Hindenburg Line in III Corps' sector had fallen and the 8th, 40th and 48th Divisions could look back with satisfaction at the manner in which they had adapted to the return of semi-open warfare. It had been a hard, wearing and very uncomfortable pursuit. One chronicler noted that:

> 'The vile weather, the mud and slush and filthy state of the ground over which the advance had to be carried out, tried to the very utmost the soldierly quality of all ranks'.[2]

The troops themselves did not of course yet know whether this was to be the end of the advance or if they were now to storm the line itself. They knew that a major offensive had opened from Arras and probably guessed that, if they were not to attack the Hindenburg Line here, they would sooner or later have to take their chance further north.

For the next six months Gonnelieu was garrisoned largely by units of the 40th Division. There were to be no large-scale attacks and the troops out on rest enjoyed a pleasant and relatively comfortable time.

A German trench mortar crew load their weapon, probably for the benefit of the cameraman.

A series of raids was conducted on the enemy outposts to the east during the summer and autumn nights and, of course, the village's houses and barns received a regular supply of gas and HE. Compared to the contemporary fury unleashed near Ypres, Gonnelieu was however a quiet, cushy sector. Although the enemy showed a similar inclination to remain fairly passive he was not prepared to allow the 40th Division to entirely dictate events; British raids always met with a resilient riposte. Whereas the British forward defences relied more on a series of unconnected posts protected by less than formidable wire, the German lines were more heavily wired and more stoutly constructed. It required greater planning and preparation for the British to get into the enemy outposts and capture a prisoner than it did for the Germans to penetrate and enter the advanced British positions. The main British defences, which incorporated Gonnelieu, were under construction further to the rear. Like the Hindenburg Line itself, these defences remained inviolate to ordinary trench raids.

Until the night of 18-19 November 1917 the 20th Division had been responsible for the village and its defences. The 12th relieved the Light Division which then shifted its divisional boundary north of the main road. Save for the passage of the 12th Division's troops and guns heading towards the newly won ground beyond the Hindenburg Line, Gonnelieu received little attention. The buildings offered largely undisturbed accommodation for the Pioneers of the 5/Northants and sappers of the 70th Field Company, both of whom nightly provided working parties and specialist skills for the infantry and gunners. The HQ of 36 Brigade was housed on the northern edge, east of the cemetery, while the north-west side provided sites for five batteries of field guns and howitzers.

The main German thrust on 30 November by the *34th* and *28th Divisions* towards Metz-en-Couture was directed up Banteux Ravine and through Gonnelieu. This was precisely the area where General Snow, GOC VII Corps, was reported to have predicted the blow would fall. So concerned was he about the vulnerability of the defences that he personally visited Villers-Guislain and ordered up 13 additional Vickers guns to cover the southern slopes of the valley and its continuation known as Twenty-Two Ravine. Snow's apprehension was similarly reflected in the concern shown by the adjoining divisional commanders, Jeudwine of the 55th and Scott of the 12th.

The 5/South Lancs on the left of the 55th Division knew little about the German onslaught before its garrisons were swept away. Similarly, the 7/Suffolk, the reserve battalion of 35 Brigade, was overwhelmed in

60

Cheshire Quarry, south-east of the village. The battalion had been subjected to a short but extremely violent bombardment of gas and HE and, despite some resistance in conjunction with five guns of the 35th MG Company positioned nearby, the Germans poured through what was the old British front line.[3] Gonnelieu itself was shelled by howitzers from about 6.45am and all communications to the rear were severed. A message from Division did get through to Brigade HQ at 8.00am ordering that the village was to be defended by any available details. The shelling was too severe to attempt to move more troops through to the eastern outskirts so the 70th Field Company was instructed to occupy Gin Avenue, a communication trench which ran east–west through the northern part of the village. It turned south-west to remain clear of the housing and about 700m west of the village it crossed the Gouzeaucourt–Gonnelieu road; here it became known as Green Switch. Two companies of the Pioneers (another company was already to the south-west of the village and later became part of Vincent's Force on Revelon Ridge) manned Green Switch and were strengthened by the arrival, complete with personal weapons, of gunners from 354th Siege Battery.

Soon after 9.00am German troops appeared in the village. Brigade HQ left its dugout and withdrew to the north-west, re-establishing itself in Farm Ravine; the gunners, RE and Pioneers remained. In the fields to the south of the Cambrai road and either side of Gin Reserve were 377th and 379th Batteries of 169 Brigade, with C Battery 63 Brigade a little behind to the west. The other two batteries of 63 Brigade were to the north of the road. The guns of 377th and 379th Batteries engaged the enemy filtering among the houses at a range of 500m. Despite many casualties the crews kept them firing until the ammunition was spent; the surviving gunners then leapt into Gin Avenue to join the RE of the Field Company. Since 5.00am C Battery of 63 Brigade had been firing on Honnecourt but, on hearing that the enemy was through to the south of Gonnelieu, ran two guns out of its pits to cover Quentin Ridge. Machine guns and shells were immediately turned on the guns which maintained a steady fire themselves on Germans seen to their right rear. Rifle fire now joined in and the battery commander and five of the six senior NCOs were killed or wounded. Under the command of Lieutenant Wallace sufficient men remained to keep two guns working – the survivors running from one gun to another to serve them alternately. The range varied from 500m to little more than 100m when a group of Germans appeared at the cemetery. The heroic, uneven fight continued for nearly two hours until, gradually, infantry of 12/RB began to reinforce the defenders of Gin Avenue. With only five men remaining, and having for the moment no more targets, Lieutenant Wallace ordered the breech blocks to be removed and the wounded evacuated. The five survivors were each awarded the DCM and Wallace the VC.

As the 4/Grenadier Guards consumed their breakfast on 30 November they received news that the Germans had taken Gonnelieu and were now marching in fours through Gouzeaucourt. The troops of 3 Guards Brigade, of which the 4/Grenadier Guards were a part, struck their bivvies and set off towards Metz-en-Couture. At 2.30pm they headed towards Gouzeaucourt expecting to have to retake the village. A little later the column again changed direction to head north and cross the Gouzeaucourt–Trescault road; here it halted a little to the north-west of the former village. General Walker, GOC 16 Brigade, visited Battalion HQ of the 4/Grenadiers to inform Lord Gort that his brigade would attack Quentin Ridge and Gonnelieu that night. He told Gort that, if the advance was unsuccessful, 3 Guards Brigade would be required to relieve the battalions of 16 Brigade and continue the assault. Subsequently at 1.00am 16 Brigade, in conjunction with 60 Brigade of the 20th Division, launched its hastily arranged operation

Ruins of Gonnelieu in 1918.

on Cemetery Ridge to the north of the Cambrai road. In the darkness and over unfamiliar ground the 2/York & Lancs and the 1/KSLI lost direction and were soon held up by heavy machine-gun fire. The 6/KSLI, and later a combined effort by the 6/Ox & Bucks and 12/RB against Gonnelieu itself, met with similarly little reward. It therefore fell upon 3 Guards Brigade to attempt what the other two brigades had failed to achieve.

Lord Gort witnessed the repulse of 16 Brigade and gloomily predicted that as he had never before seen such a machine-gun barrage as that fired against the assaulting battalions, the Guards' attack would meet with the same result. There was to be no artillery preparation and during the attack only two requisitioned field artillery brigades which happened to be passing through the area were available for support. To cap it all the promised 37 tanks of D and E Battalions, 1 Brigade, did not materialise; they either failed to find the start line or, owing to lack of petrol, never even left their assembly area. If it had not been for four machines of H Battalion, II Brigade, lent by 1 Guards Brigade, 3 Guards would have had no tank assistance at all. Nevertheless, at 6.20am with 4/Grenadier on the left and 1/Welsh on the right the brigade advanced from the railway line east of Gouzeaucourt and climbed the Quentin Ridge.

Devoid of any cover, a fury of machine-gun bullets ripped into the Guards. The Welsh were hardest hit; 248 of the 370 men who launched the assault became casualties within the first three minutes. The wounded streamed or crawled back for cover while the survivors, heads bowed as if confronting hailstones in a hurricane, pressed on. Some succeeded in gaining a trench about 60m below the summit of the ridge. Here they waited until a single tank of H Battalion waddled up to spray the German occupants of Green Switch with deadly fire. Two platoons of the Welsh immediately fought their way forward to give it assistance.

On the left the 4/Grenadier passed through the 6/Ox & Bucks of 60 Brigade who had remained out since the abortive night attack and then came across the Pioneers of the 5/Northants who had occupied the northern part of Green Switch for the previous 24 hours. On the left flank No.3 Company fought its way into the outskirts of Gonnelieu, but without artillery or tank support made little further headway. Lieutenant Hardinge established a Lewis gun in the cemetery and brought the Germans firing upon Nos.2 and 4 Companies under enfilade. The enemy were quick to react to this threat on their flank and attacked Hardinge's small party. Within a matter of seconds only he and Sergeant Hull remained unwounded; then the Lewis jammed. There was nothing more to be done so Hardinge and Hull scrambled back to safety.

Meanwhile, under intense fire, other platoons of No.3 Company penetrated the village's main street. Lieutenant Abel-Smith and Sergeant Williams made some progress but several of their party were killed when bullets pierced the brickwork of a wall they sheltered

behind. The company could get no further and withdrew. To the south-west of the village Captain Paton with No.4 Company faced a dilemma. There was no sign of the Welsh Guards to his right and No.3 on his left was withdrawing from the village. The RE of 70th Field Company and the 5/Northants on his immediate left were, in his opinion, showing signs of wavering. On four occasions Paton ran across the open, leaping from shell hole to shell hole, encouraging and exhorting the men. With machine-gun bullets howling around him his luck finally ran out and he fell mortally wounded.[4]

Captain Paton.

The Guards could get no further. At about 11.00am Brigadier Lord Henry Seymour viewed the trench held by the Welsh Guards and decided nothing more could be achieved. Lord Gort went up to make a personal reconnaissance of the situation in front of his battalion and was severely wounded in the process. Prisoners of the *14th Bavarian Reserve Regiment* and the *4th Assault Battalion* later related to their captors that a German attack originating from behind Gonnelieu was launched 30 minutes before the Guards attacked the village. They were consequently disorganised by the Guards' assault which they believed to have been a hastily arranged counter-attack. The Grenadiers concluded that even if they had captured the village, because the Welsh and the 1/Grenadier on the left were not yet up, they could not have held it. Although the fighting subsided and the new line consolidated the Grenadiers, who had lost over 200 killed and wounded, the Pioneers and the sappers of 70th Field Company were forced to wait another 24 hours before the 2/Scots Guards arrived to relieve their depleted numbers.

For the Guards Division the battle for Gonnelieu was not quite over. At 6.30am on 5 December the Germans launched two bombing raids against the 1/Irish Guards holding a front west and north-west of Gonnelieu. The Irish Guards held Green Switch and a few score yards of what had been, to the 12th Division, Gin Avenue; a bombing block in Gin Avenue divided the two armies. A barrage erupted to the rear of the Irish effectively cutting all communications to Battalion HQ and, after a well-aimed trench-mortar shell demolished the bombing block, a large force of enemy bombers entered the Guards' trench. At a cost of over 30 casualties the Irish counter-attacked and drove out the intruders to restore the status quo. The following night units of the 9th Division arrived to relieve the Guards. With a telegram of praise from Sir Douglas Haig already waiting at Divisional HQ, the survivors turned their backs on Gonnelieu and Gouzeaucourt knowing that they had, in the words of III Corps commander, maintained 'the highest traditions of the Guards'.

The 9th(Scottish)Division spent the winter months improving the forward defences and making some effort to develop the intended lines of resistance further to the rear. An anti-tank minefield of Stokes mortar bombs was laid in front of Green Switch which itself was strengthened and wired along a continuous length. Divisional defence schemes detailed that in the event of a German attack machine-gun fire would sweep the valley between Gonnelieu and Villers-Guislain while field guns would concentrate their barrage in front of the two villages. In March 1918 (26 Highland Brigade) held the division's left sector; one and a half battalions manned the Forward, with the remainder positioned further back in the Battle Zone. To their right the South African Brigade filled the defences of Gauche Wood and Quentin redoubt; to their left the 47th Division, Third Army, joined the Highlanders at Fifteen Ravine. Initially very little happened to disturb this sector of the front on 21 March. Small parties of Germans were seen to make a demonstration of debouching from Gonnelieu but, if they were serious, their advance was checked by the concentration of artillery fire upon the village. The main German thrust fell against the South Africans and the 21st Division further south. To conform with a general withdrawal to the Brown and Green Lines, the Highlanders evacuated their Battle Zone on the slope and crest facing Gonnelieu

March 1918

(See map page 57)

65

during the morning of 22 March. Seemingly unaware that the brigade had gone, the Germans were slow to pursue. In the afternoon, Scottish patrols in Gouzeaucourt heard several explosions assumed to be mines detonated by Germans emerging from their positions in Gonnelieu.

At 12.10pm on 28 September 1918 General Byng, GOC Third Army, ordered V and IV Corps to attack early next morning; their objectives were Villers-Guislain, Gonnelieu and Le Vacquerie. The operation was one element of a much larger attack which a few thousand metres to the south would take British forces through the Hindenburg Line. Two regular battalions of the Lincolnshire Regiment would attack Gonnelieu and exploit to the outpost line 2000m beyond; the 5th Division was on the left and the 6/Leicester of 110 Brigade to the right. The infantry were to advance with two tanks behind a supposedly deep, slow-moving barrage fired by four brigades of field artillery; 60-pounder guns were to concentrate their fire on Gonnelieu village. Unfortunately the operation suffered from insufficient time and planning, the consequence being that the Lincolnshire did not receive their orders until three hours before they were due to move off. The 2/Lincolnshire was to form up on a 400m front along the railway between Gouzeaucourt station and the quarry north of the Cambrai road. This was virtually the same position from where 16 Brigade had made its abortive attack on 1 December. Owing to the late arrival of orders, and gas and HE falling on Gouzeaucourt through which the battalion had to pass, the Lincolnshire did not reach the tapes before the barrage began. To the right, its 1st Battalion was in position on time and, because the 2nd was late, was allocated both available tanks. However, one machine broke down before zero and would take no part in the operation. At 3.30am the barrage, which proved to be very thin, opened on a line 1000m east of the railway. Almost immediately the two leading companies came under heavy machine-gun fire and casualties mounted. Elements of the companies did get as far as the village outskirts but to their right the 6/Leicester had been held up in front of Villers-Guislain and the 2/Lincolnshire could only get as far as Green Switch. The lone tank, *Kintore,* had trundled into the enemy lines but was then knocked out. As dawn broke the CO of the 1/Lincolnshire ordered that

> 'such men as could be should be withdrawn from their advanced positions.'[5]

Troops of the 2/Lincolnshire remained where they were, suffering for the rest of the day from the attention of enemy snipers. A later plan to envelop the village from the north over the Cambrai road was shelved when it was learnt that the 5th Division had not met with any more luck than the 21st.

In the early hours of 30 September patrols of the 2/Lincolnshire found the enemy lines still strongly held. Gonnelieu was subjected to a heavy bombardment and at about 9.00am patrols reported that the enemy had abandoned his forward positions. Sections then pushed into the village, which they discovered to be empty save for discarded equipment and some wounded men of the 1/Lincolnshire captured the previous day. The 1/Lincolnshire pushed through, secured Cheshire Quarry and then took up positions on the high ground of Banteux Spur about 800m west of the canal. Here it gained touch with the 7/Leicester which had come through Villers-Guislain. The success of a brigade of the 18th Division in reaching the canal at Vendhuile had forced the Germans to evacuate both villages. The troops of the 21st Division secured the villages and their crests and began preparations to pursue the enemy over the canal and on to the heights beyond.

Notes

1. War Diary of 2/RB. WO.95.1731
2. E.Wyrall, *The West Yorkshire Regiment*, Vol.II p.87
3. Haig's diary of 4 December noted: *'The enemy swept through the front held by the left of the 55th Division...The position is immensely strong, but the defenders seem to have put up little or no fight at all'.* The subsequent inquiry which investigated the failure of the battle concluded that the surprise had been so complete that most of the defenders were simply rounded up. It is difficult to know exactly what happened around Turner and Crook Quarries, but the 5/South Lancs did suffer 56 fatalities that day.
4. Captain George Paton MC was posthumously awarded the VC. He is buried in Metz-en-Couture Communal Cemetery British Extension.
5. War Diary of 1/Lincolnshire WO.95.2154

Gonnelieu today

While there is not much of particular interest in the village itself, its tactical importance can be appreciated by standing at the water tower on its western edge. Excellent panoramic views to the south and west give observation over Villers-Guislain, Gauche Wood and the sites of **Gonnelieu and the northern end of Quentin Ridge seen from Villers-Guislain communal cemetery. The water tower is on the left, with the dip of Twenty-Two Ravine in the centre. Cross Post, often used as a company HQ, was in the field close to the camera. The Villers-Guislain – Gonnelieu road can be seen climbing towards the three pale grain hoppers on the right.**

ATER TOWER   GRAIN HOPPERS

TWENTY-TWO RAVINE

Quentin Mill and redoubt. Gouzeaucourt and Villers-Plouich can be seen in the valleys below, with the high ground of Highland Ridge beyond to the north-west. Fusilier and Cemetery Ridges, with Welsh Ridge further on, climb towards the trees surrounding La Vacquerie. The quarry immediately east of the railway and north of the Cambrai road is today fenced off but visible behind the grey warehousing.

The ground attacked by the 4/Grenadier and 1/Welsh Guards lies below the football pitch, and the battery positions where Lieutenant Wallace won his VC are in the fields on the other side of the road running past the water tower (D96). The communal cemetery contains only one known British grave, that of Lance-Corporal Abernethy, 4/Grenadier Guards, who probably died on 1 December. Seven other graves were later lost and are commemorated by a memorial in Villers Hill British Cemetery.

The chateau was rebuilt, but like many in this area is more chateau in name than reality. To the east the motorway passes beneath the D96 at just about the position of the Hindenburg Line. By turning sharp right on entering Banteux the motorist can follow a small road which cuts along Banteux Ravine and up to Villers-Guislain. Immediately after the motorway bridge and despite the dumping of recent spoil, the sites of Turner and Crook Quarries can still be discerned. After the quarries a track joins the road from the right. This continues up the ravine and meets a cross track 600m along at the site of Cheshire Quarry. The left track climbs up to Villers-Guislain and joins the minor road from Banteux. Here it becomes *Rue Julien Plé*. The right track climbs up to Gonnelieu and becomes *Rue Verte*. Interesting as these tracks are, they are usually impassable by ordinary car.

The north-western edge of Gauche Wood on the left and the trees which now surround the site of Quentin Mill on the right, as seen from Gonnelieu water tower. Quentin redoubt was sited roughly mid way between the two. The Villers-Guislain – Gouzeaucourt road runs in the valley and climbs towards Quentin Mill. The camera looks across the land traversed by Green Switch and the area in which Captain George Paton won his VC.

GAUCHE WOOD   QUENTIN MILL

Chapter Four

EAST OF EPEHY

The village of Epéhy was captured by the 48th Division in March and April 1917. Posts across the spurs and valleys to the east of the village were gradually extended towards the Hindenburg Line. One such operation took place on a wicked night in mid-April. At 11.30pm, in zero visibility and into the teeth of a howling gale, the 5/Warwick set off towards Catelet Copse and Little Priel Farm. The conditions were against them and the attack failed; one day later, the Germans voluntarily abandoned the two positions. Further south the Germans were determined to fight for possession of the ridges, but in the sector between Honnecourt and Vendhuile, as for example at Little Priel Farm where the land fell away to the canal, the British enjoyed observation over the German positions. The 48th and 42nd Divisions established themselves in the posts and eventually a consolidated and reasonably connected trench system developed to the rear. In May 1917, Brigadier-General V.A.Ormsby was killed in Catelet Copse as he

Spring 1917

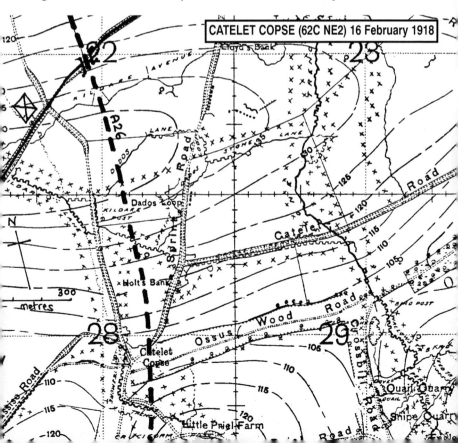

CATELET COPSE (62C NE2) 16 February 1918

inspected what was to become the new front line for 127 Brigade. A brigade of the 8th Division spent a short time in the sector until it was relieved by units of 3 and 5 Cavalry Brigades.

Compared with the activity to the north-west near Arras and Bullecourt, the area east of Epéhy was relatively quiet. However, as the summer months wore on, raids and patrols increased in both size and frequency. The Germans raided the Birdcage, an advanced British post connected to Quail Quarry by a single communication trench, on 28 May and captured the unfortunate Corporal Dunn of the North Somerset Yeomanry. Three weeks later, when it was held by the Leicestershire Yeomanry, the enemy again raided the position. The cavalry were not prepared to remain only on the receiving end and in a retaliatory action in mid-June the Royals raided an enemy post near Ossus Wood. A more ambitious attempt was made on 25 June by the Royal Dragoons, accompanied by men from the 3rd Dragoon Guards, the North Somerset Yeomanry and the 3rd Field Squadron. Two parties comprising 100 men set off to attack posts between Canal Wood and Ossus Wood. Travelling either side of Cox's Road, the troops crossed the 750m of No Man's Land, on compass bearing, through five feet high thistles. The barrage was good, but sufficient German rifle and trench-mortar fire hampered the troopers as they approached the enemy wire. As they struggled to fire a Bangalore torpedo, Lieutenant John Dunville shielded the men of the Field Squadron with his own body. Initially, the Bangalore failed to explode and when it was eventually persuaded to work, it was almost time for the raiders to withdraw. They identified men of the 2nd Battalion, 124th Infantry Regiment and then withdrew, taking their wounded with them. Lieutenant Dunville died of wounds at Villers-Faucon the following day and was subsequently awarded a posthumous VC. Lieutenant Helme was also buried in the same cemetery. Soon after it moved into the area, 104 Brigade of the 35th Division was also ordered to conduct a major raid. Undertaken by three battalions on 21 August, it was designed to be something of a diversion from the main divisional attack against the Knoll and Gillemont Farm. The 23/Manchester and

Lieutenant Dunville

17/Lancashire Fusiliers (both battalions had lost their 'bantam' status earlier in the year) attacked the same stretch of German line as 6 Cavalry Brigade had done in June. These woods lay just to the north and south of the hamlet of Ossus, immediately west of the canal. Tension and activity in the area had been increasing in recent weeks: in late June an enemy raid had captured a newly arrived sergeant of the

23/Manchester and another in mid-July was repelled only with some difficulty. Besides substantial casualties to the 15/Sherwood Foresters, this raid caused 12 dead and 23 wounded among a company of the 19/Northumberland Fusiliers, the divisional Pioneers. The company had been sent up to the Birdcage to assist the garrison and suffered from the heavy German bombardment put down to cover the raiders' withdrawal.

The raid by 104 Brigade in August was intended to get men into Hawke and Canal Wood Trenches, spend about 25 minutes bombing dugouts and then get back across No Man's Land with a bag of enemy prisoners. Because the wire in front of the enemy trenches was reported to be fairly thin, it was decided to rely on a barrage starting at about the same time as the raiders began their assault. When the raid began, the 17/LF discovered that instead of a negligible obstacle, the wire consisted of two belts of apron, each about 15 feet deep, and one of concertina.

Zero was 4.25am. The 23/Manchester sent over 14 officers and 259 other ranks, a substantial raiding party, organised into four groups. Twenty-five minutes before they jumped off, the Manchesters endured a severe barrage put down by the enemy in response to an SOS from the Knoll. Nevertheless, they fought their way through the wire and into the German trenches stretching 300m either side of Catelet Road. The post-raid report recorded 'severe casualties'[1] inflicted upon the enemy. When the whistles ordering withdrawal were blown, the raiders charged back up the slope and into the relative safety of their own trenches.

Just to the north of the Manchesters, the Fusiliers had formed up near Lone Tree, a few hundred yards to the west of Cox's Road. Wearing roses in their helmets in remembrance of Minden Day, they hacked their way through the wire and forced a passage to a bank some 200m west of the main Vendhuile-Honnecourt Road. Here they captured 11 prisoners, killed a number of Germans and blew in several dugouts with Stokes mortar bombs.

To maintain pressure on the enemy and divert some of his attention away from the attack on the Knoll and beyond, the 20/LF carried out a raid on the evening of the same day. Having learnt from the difficulties experienced by their comrades in 104 Brigade, the Fusiliers went over after a battery of 6-inch howitzers had fired into the wire. The objectives were German lines in *les Tranchées*, a much contested area just outside Honnecourt on the Epéhy road. The ground sloped down Seventeen Spur towards the objective, again giving the British the

See map
page 72

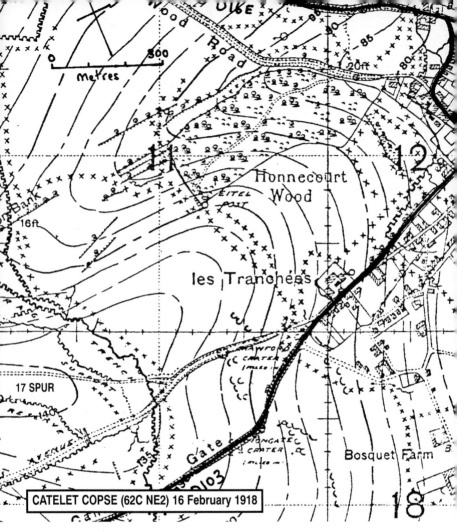

CATELET COPSE (62C NE2) 16 February 1918

advantage of the land. The raiding party consisted of Captain Cressy and two lieutenants, with 64 other ranks. Despite the bombardment however, the raiders experienced difficulty in getting through the wire. A Bangalore torpedo blew one gap and other troops crossed the wire by means of mats. The German trenches were discovered to be empty, and after 12 minutes of exploration the raiders retired. They reorganised behind a bank 20m from the German trenches and then dashed back through enemy machine-gun fire and a trench mortar barrage. A later report stated that the men were in 'excellent spirits'[2] and that they 'much regretted' that they had not been able to get at the enemy.

Raiding parties from three battalions had successfully entered the

Bosquet Farm, seen from the area known as les Tranchées. This was the land crossed by units of 104 Brigade during their raid on the German lines in August 1917.

enemy trenches and had captured prisoners belonging to the *10th Bavarian Division*. Furthermore, they had not suffered too severely themselves. The 23/Manchester sustained the highest number of casualties: seven dead, one died of wounds and 48 wounded. The 17/LF lost four dead and its sister battalion, one. The 204th Field Company, some of whose sappers went over with the 20/LF, also lost one man killed. The enterprise had probably not affected the outcome for the struggle going on two miles to the south, but it had demonstrated the division's ability to conduct coordinated trench raids.

November 1917

The 35th Division was next sent north to the Salient, being replaced later in the Epéhy sector by the 55th Division. This division had suffered a severe mauling during the summer and autumn battles for the Flanders ridges. It was too weak to do anything other than to simulate a diversionary attack involving dummy tanks, dummy men and a great deal of gas, during the opening stages of the Cambrai offensive. The German counter-attack of 30 November was preceded by a barrage which rolled and swelled in its intensity and by flights of low-flying aircraft which machine gunned the unfortunate 55th Division. The enemy's first break through on this, the left of their attack, occurred on 165 Brigade's front at Eagle Quarry. Supported from the rear by a section of D/276th Battery firing from near Little Priel farm, the 6/King's fought on until their ammunition was exhausted. Even then, and despite receiving fire from aircraft, 4.2-inch shells and small arms fire, Sergeant C.Gurley and another gunner kept at least one of their howitzers firing until the enemy switched his thrust to 165 Brigade a little to the north. For his tenacity and bravery, Gurley was awarded the VC.

In the early morning of 30 November Pigeon Quarry was held by the 10/King's of 166 Brigade. The quarry had been developed into something of a strong point but the German bombardment and infantry assault were so overwhelming that few of the Liverpool Scottish escaped to continue the fight from posts further back. Some of the garrison successfully reached Limerick Post where, until nightfall with members of the 5/King's Own and the 5/LNL, they resisted further attacks. One company of the 5/King's Own defended Meath Post, 1000m north of Limerick, and was forced to withdraw to the south where it joined with some of the 6/King's of 166 Brigade west of Little Priel Farm. The division's reserve brigade was rushed up from Villers-Faucon and Longavesnes; one of its battalions, the 4/King's Own dug in to the rear of Limerick Post. It was joined later by the 8/King's who extended the line towards Vaucellette Farm. Here, amid the confusion caused by broken communications and the general 'fog of war', it made contact with some Northumberland Hussars.

In a desperate attempt to regain some of the lost ground and halt the enemy counter-attack, cavalry of the Mhow Brigade (4th Cavalry Division) were thrown into the offensive. On 1 December the 2/Lancers, a squadron of the 6th (Inniskilling) Dragoons and a section of the 11th Machine Gun Squadron left Epéhy from the east, crossed the railway and galloped down Catelet Valley. There had been some initial delay because as the Lancers had been detailed to go into the trenches dismounted they moved up to the assembly area

Lance-Dafadar Gobind Singh

without lances. These were hurriedly brought forward, distributed and the advance began. The cavalry came under fire from machine guns on both sides of the valley and from Kildare Trench across their front. The OC of the Lancers was killed during the charge, but the regiment pressed on, some jumping the wire protecting Kildare Trench while others struggled through gaps. The Germans fled, pursued by the Lancers who killed approximately 15 Germans with the lance and 20 with rifles. However, the charge was eventually halted by machine-gun fire, and the Lancers regrouped in Kildare Trench and around Kildare Post. Some horses were held in a sunken lane in advance of the occupied positions, while others were led back to the rear. One weak company of the 6/King's of 165 Brigade

German machine gun team.

managed to get up and occupied a position to the south of Catelet Copse. They were followed by two dismounted squadrons of the 38th Central India Horse, sent forward to reinforce, or if necessary, extricate the 2/Lancers. Two mounted sowars of the CIH galloped up to Kildare Lane (a communication trench) to see if it was occupied by the Germans, jumped it, turned their horses around and galloped back to report not only was it fully manned, but that it also contained several machine guns. Meanwhile their dismounted colleagues had been halted by fire from Limerick Post; after sustaining over 50 casualties they were forced to retire.

Further forward, Lance-Dafadar Gobind Singh volunteered to carry back messages from the Lancers' advanced position in Kildare Trench. Under heavy fire, he made the journey to the regimental report centre three times, having a horse shot from under him on each trip. Singh was awarded the VC. The Lancers maintained a determined defence of their positions throughout the day, making use of captured German grenades and even trying to advance on foot towards Pigeon Ravine. In the late afternoon the cavalry was ordered to retire and, having shot their wounded horses and accompanied by some stragglers of the 55th Division, returned down Catelet Valley. Men of the 21st Division passed in the opposite direction and occupied most of the positions won earlier in the day. The cost to the cavalry had been grim. Besides those casualties sustained by the CIH, the Lancers lost five British and three Indian officers and 105 other ranks. However, the Germans had also had enough for the time being and the line quietened down.

During the winter the 16th Division moved into the area. The weather was appalling but the Irish began to make their contribution to the continuing development of the defence lines. Considerable energy was expended on, among others, Mule Trench, Heythorp Post and Little Priel Farm. Some posts had become so untenable that several were abandoned and the outpost line withdrawn a little from the positions reached by the Lancers and the 55th Division, westwards down Catelet, Deelish and St Patrick's Valleys. This did not mean all aggressive activity on the part of the British ceased. Patrols of the 1/Royal Dublin Fusiliers frequently investigated Catelet Copse and a raid by the 2/Munster on Kildare Post during the night of 15-16 March

**March
1918**

Targelle Ravine Cemetery, with the trees of Villers Hill Cemetery on the ridge above. Gloster Road, which was 'choked with dead' in September 1918, can be seen climbing the hill between the two cemeteries.

bagged a talkative German who declared that his division was about to be relieved by another. This new division, he insisted, was being brought in to spearhead an attack. On the night of 19-20 March a patrol of two officers and 30 men of the 2/RDF left Grafton Post and entered the German trenches north of Lark Post. At least six enemy were killed. It was not, however, all one sided. The Germans launched a strong raid on Heythorp Post in February when it was held by the 1/RDF; another in early March by nearly 50 raiders, again against the 1/RDF, resulted in several casualties. On 21 March the enemy storm troops were so close behind their barrage that these outposts fell in the first few minutes of the attack.

By mid-September 1918, the 58th Division had fought some very hard engagements to get through and beyond Peiziere. German resistance in front of the Hindenburg Line remained severe and all ground won in the approaches to Catelet Copse and Ossus Wood was fiercely contested. On 21 September an attack by the 2/10 and 12/London towards Limerick and Kildare Posts, was brought to a bloody end by German machine-gunners. A simultaneous attack by 19 Brigade to their north against Meath Post and the ground immediately north of Limerick Post, also failed. The 5/Scottish Rifles tried again in the evening of 21 September, managing to secure and hang on to Meath Post. The 1/Wiltshire of 110 Brigade had captured the post three days earlier but had been forced to abandon it when troops on the flanks failed to keep up. The failure of the initial attack by 19 Brigade prompted one officer to observe that 'the young drafts appeared to have lost their mastery over the rifle'. The troops who attacked the northern end of Gloster Road were 'mercilessly mown down' and at the end of the day the road was 'choked with dead'.[3]

The Queen Victoria's Rifles were ordered to reopen the attack on Kildare Post. In view of the fact that the enemy had the advantage of higher ground, the battalion petitioned Brigade that the operation should be done at night. Brigade HQ sanctioned the request and while the QVR attacked Kildare Post from the west, the divisional Pioneers (4/Suffolk) attacked north from Catelet Copse. Under a creeping barrage the two battalions attacked and captured the heavily defended posts. The enemy fled, abandoning many weapons, rations and packs. At mid-day on 22 September, and using thistles as camouflage to creep within 50 yards of the post, the Germans launched a counter-attack against the Queen Victoria's. A fierce bombing engagement followed until the enemy was driven off. Another German attack by about 50 men from the 2nd Guards Division came down Sprint Road under the cover of its substantial bank. The Germans penetrated Dados Lane and Dados Loop, but carrying parties of the Rangers brought up more bombs for the Queen Vics and the enemy was forced back. Sergeant Hart and Rifleman Rossi were both awarded Military Medals for their bravery when coping with the German bombers. The 2/Worcester had made a converging attack on Limerick Post earlier that morning. Slipping and stumbling on the wet dew, the troops rushed forward to discover the Germans had abandoned the post.

During the night of 23-24 September, the London Division was withdrawn and the 12th, which was equally exhausted having hammered its way through Epéhy, extended its front to the north. On 21 September the 6/West Kent had attempted to take Little Priel Farm, but despite five desperate assaults, the enemy held on, supported by

A Lewis gun team of the 1st or 2nd Lincoln about to go into action east of Epéhy, 18 September 1918. IWM Q11327

intense fire from two posts to the south - Grafton[4] and Heythorp. Eventually, the Kents' lieutenant-colonel came up and, with only five men, stormed Grafton. A little to the north, the objectives of 36 Brigade were Cruciform and Cottesmore Posts. This attack was held up by machine-gun fire from Little Priel Farm; the 9/RF suffered more than 280 casualties. At midnight, and in bright moonlight, the 5/Berkshire charged the farm with the bayonet, captured it and took 40 machine guns as trophies.

Fighting remained severe for several days. The enemy persistently attacked Dados Lane and Dados Loop, positions which allowed superb observation over the Hindenburg Line and enemy posts to the south. The need for the British to press on became greater on 26 September when the division received information that the US 27th Division was to attack the Hindenburg Line on its right the following day. Patrols pushed forward towards Ossus Wood, but Lark Post and the Quarries remained strongly held. In the early morning of 27 September, the 6/Buffs attacked the Quarries, taking over 150 prisoners in the process. On the left, the 6/West Kent advanced on Swallow and Catelet Trenches, but did not secure them until late in the day. Early the following morning, the remaining stretch of Dados Lane finally fell. This allowed patrols to push on to Ossus Wood without being overlooked from the left. The 6/Buffs linked up with the 18th Division and reached the western outskirts of Vendhuile. After all the trouble it

See map on page 69

Activity at the 65th Field Ambulance, 21st Division, near Epéhy on 18 September 1918. German prisoners and British wounded await evacuation to the rear

had taken to get there, the battalion was disgruntled to be attacked next by an American tank. CSM Smith hammered on the hull with his rifle butt until the crew was persuaded to stop firing. On the left of the 12th Division, 98 and 100 Brigades of the 33rd had also fought their way to the canal. Both brigades had suffered badly in the early hours of 29 September because their attack was scheduled to commence before that of the 12th. The hope was that a subsidiary attack down Targelle Valley towards Ossus would distract the German artillery on La Terriere plateau from firing on the 12th, 18th, 27th (American) and 46th Divisions. Because the greater proportion of the British guns was to be used to support the attack to the south, the 33rd knew its artillery support would be inadequate. Brigadier-General Baird (100 Brigade) protested that this lack of support and his brigade's early start would result in disaster. Division told him to get on with the job and to stop complaining.

The objectives of the 2/Worcester were Gloster Road and Pigeon Trench. At 5.30am the battalion advanced from Limerick Trench and once again found the dew and recent rain had made the going difficult. It soon lost the sparse barrage and was cut down in swathes by machine guns in Gloster Road and the crossroads on its right. The survivors crept back under a descending mist to Limerick Trench. Here they became the intermittent target of German guns for the remainder of the day. With the successful advance by the 12th Division on its right, the battalion pushed out patrols next morning. Gloster Road and Pigeon Trench were both empty. The Worcesters discovered their own dead heaped in front of the sunken road and in an arc before the crossroads. They had lost eight subalterns and nearly 80 killed. The officers were buried together near the crossroads and many of the other ranks interred nearby. The battalion was understandably very bitter at the lack of artillery support. However, it was later informed that its sacrifice had diverted enemy guns from targets further south and that a fresh division had been sent up to reinforce the *Jaeger* units in front of the 33rd Division. The remaining 200 men, who comprised the trench strength of the battalion, linked up with the 12th Division on the canal on 30 September.

Notes

1. War Diary of 23/Manchester, 21 August 1917. WO.95.2484
2. War Diary of 20/Lancashire Fusiliers, 21 August 1917. WO.2484
3. G.Hutchinson, *The 33rd Division 1915-1919*, p.129
4. On some 1918 maps, probably through a cartographical error, Grafton Post became Braeton Post.

The area east of Epéhy today.

This large area of good arable land rolls gently towards the canal. Intersected by shallow valleys and dotted with small copses, a network of headlands and farm tracks traverse the undulating fields. Distinctive features are few and sporadic, but by taking particular notice of church towers, radio masts, cemeteries and farms, visitors can keep their bearings.

Several of the smaller copses in Deelish Valley were not regrown and Catelet Copse is now under the motorway. Little Priel Farm is one of the few buildings of any size in the locality. Although the farmhouse itself is a well-structured building, parts of it are little better than they appeared in 1917. It stands aloof above the fields, shielded from the motorway by its outbuildings and encompassing trees. The maze of trenches south of the farm has been ploughed over and the track which originally connected Heythorp Post with the Quarries has also disappeared. A line of trees follows its route. Eagle Quarry lies in a valley bottom on the minor road between the farm and Vendhuile. What was once the scene of frantic activity and frequent raids is now a slurry dump. Snipe and Quail Quarries also remain but are heavily overgrown. There is no longer access past them into Ossus Wood or to the site of the Birdcage.

Ossus Wood has regrown in almost the same shape as it was in 1914. Its hamlet is a pretty collection of houses near the junction of Catelet and Cox's Road with the Vendhuile-Honnecourt road. Bosquet Farm, between Ossus and Honnecourt, is a large imposing farm beneath the slope of Seventeen Spur. Honnecourt village straddles both sides of the canal. It nestles beneath some rocky cliffs which provided

The beautifully compact Pigeon Ravine Cemetery. German storm troops swept across the rolling mist-shrouded hills behind in March 1918. In September, British troops found them considerably harder going.

The war memorial at Villers-Guislain. The plinth includes the names of three villagers thought to have been killed by an unearthed shell in April 1920.

accommodation and storage for the Germans during their occupation. A well-maintained grotto to Notre Dame de Lourdes, complete with candles and statues, was carved into one of the outcrops following a village visit to the shrine in 1935. To the west, the land climbs steeply from this sleepy village up to Villers Ridge.

Some of the roads have kept their banks while others are now merely tracks across fields. The area has an unexpected beauty. The monotony of the crops is occasionally relieved by a bank or line of trees which offer a contrasting splash of colour. The motorway is largely hidden by trees or a cutting and does little to detract from the rural ambiance. Grain silos and water towers add some artificial dimension to the otherwise usually discreet gatherings of buildings.

The area contains four British cemeteries: Pigeon Ravine, Meath, Targelle Ravine and Villers Hill.

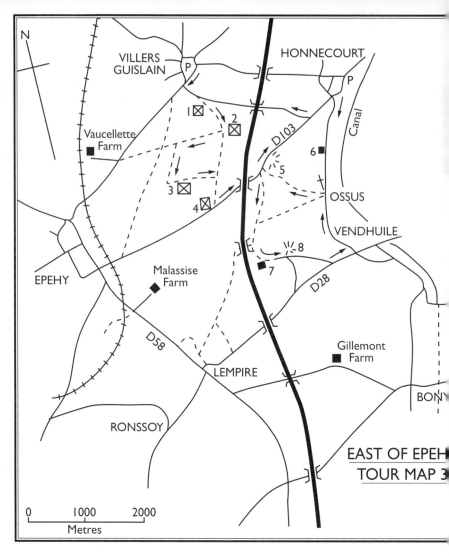

N

VILLERS
GUISLAIN

HONNECOURT

P

P

1 ⊠

2 ⊠

D103

6 ■

Vaucellette
Farm ■

Canal

5

3 ⊠

4 ⊠

OSSUS

VENDHUILE

EPEHY

Malassise
Farm ◆

8

7 ■

D28

D58

Gillemont
Farm ■

LEMPIRE

BONY

RONSSOY

EAST OF EPEH

TOUR MAP 3

0   1000   2000
Metres

Pigeon Ravine Cemetery. The eight officers of the 2/Worcester killed on 29
September were buried together close to where they fell. The graves of
their men are in the main plot.

In its lonely, exposed position, Meath Cemetery sits above Targelle and Pigeon Ravines. It is rarely visited, but the walk to its dominating position is well worth the effort.

East of Epéhy: Tour 1
(Tour Map 3)
9.7kms, 6 miles. 2.75 hours

Park in front of the *Mairie* at Villers-Guislain. Head south on the main street and turn left at the CWGC signs. Continue down the road and fork right at the sign towards Villers Hill British Cemetery. (1)

Follow the track down to Targelle Ravine Cemetery. (2) Take the track which runs along the valley bottom. After 1000m turn left up the tarmac and climb up from Quail Ravine. (If time is of the essence, there is an earlier track which goes up to Meath Cemetery.) The tarmac ends 800m on. Turn left and follow the headland along to Meath Cemetery. (3)

After visiting the cemetery turn right to continue along the grass baulk. At 700m it joins Gloster Road. Turn right and walk along to Pigeon Ravine Cemetery. (4) Turn left onto the road and go under the motorway. Follow the road up past Pigeon Quarry (5) and, just before

These close-packed graves of men from the 2/Argyll & Sutherland Highlanders in Villers Hill Cemetery indicate the haste with which they were originally buried.

you enter Honnecourt, turn sharp left onto a minor road back to Villers-Guislain. This junction was the site of Crawford Crater. This minor road climbs up Seventeen Spur and offers marvellous views across the country to Bony church, Gillemont Farm, Vaucellette Farm, Birdwood Copse, Gauche Wood and Villers-Guislain church. This road crosses the motorway and returns past the track leading down to Villers Hill Cemetery.

Tour 2

10.8kms, 6.75miles. 2.75 hours

Park in Honnecourt village. Take the road towards Vendhuile running parallel to the canal. Pass Bosquet Farm on the right (6) and the area where Lieutenant Dunville won his VC. Pass the *Hameau d'Ossus* sign and 700m further on turn right at the crucifix and house number 28. This track (Cox's Road) climbs quite sharply and then drops down past an abandoned caravan to Targelle Valley by means of a recently cleared sunken lane. Follow the track over the (sometime) stream and join the D103.

Turn left at the road and left again at a track after 200m. This was known as Sprint Road. Follow this up to the crest to enjoy the views and descend past Dados Loop. Catelet Road joins from the left but continue down to the valley bottom by the motorway underpass. Bear left (keeping east of the motorway), climb up past Little Priel Farm (7) and drop down past the Quarries. (8) Continue to the western outskirts of the village of Vendhuile and turn left onto the Honnecourt road. It passes the eastern end of Ossus Wood. Return by this road to your car.

Chapter Five

RONSSOY AND LEMPIRE

On 27 August 1914 elements of the 2nd Cavalry Division and 10 Brigade passed through Lempire on their way south. It is possible that some 'old sweats' of the 2/Royal Dublin Fusiliers who were in that column returned to the village in late 1917 when their battalion, then part of the 16th Division, took up residence amongst its ruins. On this occasion it was not going to be merely a march through yet another anonymous French village, but the battalion's virtual Golgotha.

On 1 April 1917 patrols of the 48th Division extended down the road from Epéhy towards Lempire. Apart from the capture of Malassise Farm by the 7/Worcester, they made little progress. On 5 April, with the 4/Berkshire on the left, 4/Ox & Bucks in the centre and 5/Gloucester on the right, 145 Brigade made a concerted attack on

A British howitzer and crew take advantage of the shelter of a partly destroyed wall as they follow the withdrawal across the devastated zone in 1917.

Ronssoy. There was no preliminary artillery bombardment but the enemy seemed to be expecting the attack and put one of their own down at 5.00pm. Fortunately it fell on the lines the attacking battalions had already left, but the South Midlanders did not have it easy. The protecting wire was discovered to be thick, and deep snow lay on the streets and shrouded the tumbled ruins. After some severe street

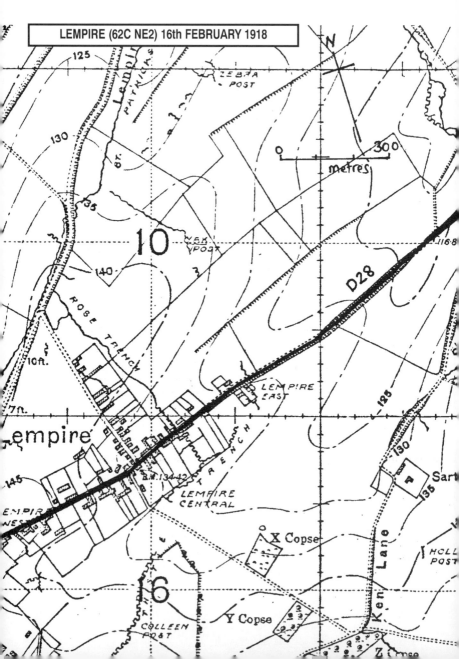

LEMPIRE (62C NE2) 16th FEBRUARY 1918

fighting, the two villages were taken. The *Official History* later expressed the belief that this was probably one of the war's few operations where the attackers suffered fewer casualties than the defenders. The capture of the devastated villages was an important achievement for the British as it gave them possession of the ridge in front of the Hindenburg Line. Wary of the booby traps left by the Germans, the South Midlanders began to consolidate the two villages. The 6/Gloucester suffered a grievous blow on 18 April when a device, which was either triggered or time-fused, exploded in Battalion HQ. The CO and the Adjutant, two brothers from Stoke Bishop, were killed, along with the battalion's Medical Officer, Chaplain and a subaltern.

In early May the 42nd Division relieved the 48th. The Midlanders went up to the Bullecourt area where they became involved on the periphery of that particular battle. The 42nd Division had spent seven months on Gallipoli and, since the evacuation, had been conducting desert operations against the Turks in Egypt. Consequently, the men suffered badly from the extreme change in temperature. The weather was still snowy and very cold but as the weather warmed up the Lancastrians began to acclimatize and increased their patrols. Like the 48th, they lost several men through delayed-action booby traps. Captain Baird, MO of the 10/Manchester, was killed when one such mine went up in Longavesnes and other officers had a narrow escape when a quantity of explosives was found attached to a beam in one of their billets. Losses were not high, although 50 men of the 6th and 7/LF were buried when a shell collapsed the cellars in Malassise Farm. Patrolling and constant work on improving and extending the trench lines cost more casualties, but the major activity was taking place a little to the south.

During its summer stay in the Lempire sector the 35th Division's main concern was to improve the British positions around the Knoll and Gillemont Farm. Lempire and Ronssoy were garrisoned and some work done to extend the fairly sparse defences. Battalions holding the sector conducted raids and active patrols and the villages themselves were often the target of German guns. In late summer and autumn, units of the former 2nd Cavalry Division returned to garrison the scene of their short 1914 engagement near Lempire. They were followed in November by West Lancashire Territorials of the 55th Division.

The already sorely tried battalions of the 55th were stretched to the limit when the German counter-attack fell on its front on 30 November. Its outposts were forced back and dispositions rapidly improvised to prevent the fall of the high ground around Lempire and Ronssoy. The

November 1917

9/King's, already deployed in the Lempire defences, was moved northwards towards May and Quid Copses and replaced by one company of Pioneers of the 4/South Lancs, the 423rd Field Company and elements of the 180th Tunnelling Company. The 2/5 LF subsequently arrived from Villers-Faucon to prolong the line from May Copse to Malassise Farm. In due course they were joined by the remainder of the Pioneer battalion and two more Field Companies. This assorted collection of units extended the line north of the farm and remained in support to the 4/King's Own and the 8/King's. Two battalions of the 24th Division, who, although under heavy gas and HE bombardment, had not been attacked, were deployed behind the over-extended 55th Division in support. The extremely weak battalions remained under pressure for the remainder of the day but maintained their existing positions until the German storm subsided.

The combination of a very reduced strength resulting from its heavy losses during Third Ypres, dislocation caused by the German counter-attack and the severe cold of December 1917 meant that the 55th Division had managed to do little permanent work on the Lempire trenches. The Irish too could do little until the thaw began in January.

German cavalry advance over British defences on 22 March 1918. Note the Lewis gun and its dead gunner.

When it did arrive, and despite further sporadic snow falls and the problem of collapsing trenches, the division was put to work. The 8/9 Royal Dublin Fusiliers began work on 18 posts which were to constitute the Lempire and Ronssoy Defences. The Fusiliers cleared out old trenches, dug cruciform posts and laid inordinate amounts of wire. Battalions in brigade support daily sent out parties of at least 200 to dig and, at times, two complete companies could be dispatched to the construction sites. For several days the 1/RDF took advantage of the heavy mist in mid-February to have all available men digging on Ridge Reserve. Gradually, the semblance of a defensive structure for the villages took shape. However, despite all the work done during the winter months, one officer of the 2/Leinster later recalled that front line trenches remained very shallow, that there was insufficient wire and that, although the maps suggested a defence scheme in depth, in reality there was little behind the Battle Zone except open space. Furthermore, when the GOC, General Hull, complained to General Gough that his order to maintain five battalions in the front line and one in the Battle Zone would result in severe casualties and probably lead to the fall of the Battle Zone, Gough refused to sanction Hull's suggested scheme of redeployment.

No doubt other officers of the division agreed with Hull and at least one, Major Harrison of the 2/Royal Irish Regiment, later complained of the inadequate defensive system and of Gough's orders concerning deployment. Harrison, whose battalion was all but annihilated on 21 March, thundered:

> 'a more formidable resistance could have been put up had all the battalion commanders in the line been able to keep a reserve of two companies in the Red Line and make a continuous strong line of resistance'.[1]

He criticised the absence of defence in depth, insisting that brigades should have deployed one battalion in the Forward Zone, one in the Battle Zone and another in support. This, Harrison stressed, would have been preferable to having a heavy concentration in the forward posts where, as a result of the mist, their machine guns proved to be largely useless. The bulk of these weapons, like the bulk of the troops, should have been in the Battle Zone.

While it attempted to prepare for what many considered to be the inevitable German onslaught, the 16th, like other divisions of the BEF, was undergoing quite dramatic change. The reduction of brigades to three battalions resulted in the 6/RIR, 8/9 RDF and 10/RDF being disbanded and the 2/Leinster arriving from the 24th Division.

Although the disbanded units dispatched their personnel to other battalions in the division, several units appear to have remained considerably under strength. For example, in late February the 2/Munster claimed a trench strength of only 25 officers and 487 other ranks.

The infantry brigades remained composed of Irish battalions but the division retained its non-Irish anomaly - the 11/Hampshire (Pioneers). Having lost over 100 of its most physically fit men to the 1/Hants and receiving a smaller number of B1 men in return, this very English battalion was also undergoing change. After three years of attachment to the division the battalion had become accustomed to the Irish and, although it seems not to have actually received an issue of shamrocks on 17 March, apparently happily joined in the singing of Irish songs. Not all the battalions were quite as happy with the arrangements for St Patrick's Day, and several small demonstrations of discontent occurred.[2] Furthermore, at the same time as the often morale-sapping personnel changes were taking place, the division received a new GOC. The disruptions to the division had not of course prevented the units from performing the normal routines of trench warfare. One company of the 1/Munster had raided two trenches between the Knoll and Gillemont Farm, capturing five prisoners. For two days after the raid the enemy was reported to be regularly hurling bombs at his own wire; the Munsters had made him 'decidedly nervous and jumpy'.

**March
1918**

Shielded by the mist, on 21 March the Germans penetrated the area of 49 Brigade, and stormed position after position. 49 Brigade's right battalion, the 7/RIR, had two companies in the front posts and two in support at Ronssoy. Very few of their garrisons managed to escape to the rear and the two support companies were practically surrounded before they realised the Germans were through to their front and right. All the officers except one became casualties: ten were captured and seven were reported missing. One of the captured was Second Lieutenant Hadden. Hadden's platoon manned the trenches near Gillemont Farm. With all telephone lines cut, Hadden sent back his signallers and then tried to escape. He bumped into some Germans, was captured and then slipped away. He scrambled into Duncan Post and gave the alarm, before setting off to report to the Red Line. He was again captured and once more escaped. He next managed to get to Sart Farm, just in time for it to be taken by the Germans. On this occasion he remained captured. The 7th's sole remaining officer and about 40 other ranks fought a delaying action in a trench running between Ronssoy and its wood, but withdrew when fired upon from the rear. A group of Inniskillings had attached themselves to this party, which succeeded in struggling back to Ste Emilie. The 7/8 Royal Inniskilling Fusiliers was 49 Brigade's support battalion in Ronssoy. Lieutenant-Colonel Walkley and most of his HQ staff were killed or captured.

One German thrust turned north to roll up the 16th's line while another forged on to the west. Assisted by a party from their 2nd Battalion, one platoon of the 7/RIR held on to Z Copse until 3.00pm but, with Sart Farm to its north and Queuchettes Wood to the south having fallen by 11.00am, Battalion HQ of 2/RIR decided to burn the official papers and joined forces with about 15 of the 7th Battalion men who had escaped from Gillemont Farm. This group occupied a trench running from Bassè Boulogne to Colleen Post. The enemy was through either side of the trench and gradually the troops filtered back to Irish Trench on Bellicourt Road. An enemy machine gun was already ensconced in the southern end of this trench. Despite silencing the gun, at 2.30pm the group began to retire on Ste Emilie. As it began to withdraw, another machine gun about 300m away to its left opened up on the fleeing party. Only about three officers and 15 men reached the comparative safety of Ste Emilie. With some managing to hold out late into the afternoon, the battalion's remaining posts continued their resistance until the defenders were killed or captured. One post near the wireless station in Ronssoy was still reported to be holding out on 22 March. The 2nd Battalion's casualties for the day were recorded as Lieutenant-Colonel Scott killed, 17 officers and 499 other ranks missing. **(See map pages 86)**

Two battalions of the reserve brigade, the 1/Munster and 2/Leinster, along with the Pioneers were ordered up from Villers-Faucon to Ste Emilie. All three battalions lost considerable numbers from shelling but remained in touch with each other and with the left flank of the 66th Division. They held their positions throughout the night but in the early morning the Germans renewed their assault. Covered by the Pioneers who 'put up a very fine fight',[3] the brigade withdrew on Villers-Faucon. Even the Munsters, who had not of course been manning the Forward or Battle Zones, lost 17 officers and 500 men during the course of 21-22 March.

At about the same time as the Munsters, the Leinsters and Hants had gone into the trenches near Ste Emilie, the other battalion of 47 Brigade, the 6/Connaught Rangers, had been ordered to counter-attack the sugar factory to the west of Ronssoy. Subsequent word cancelling the attack failed to reach the Rangers in time. They attacked without the promised support of either the artillery or another battalion. The brave effort was stopped by enfilade fire and strafing from low-flying aircraft.

The three regular battalions of 48 Brigade fared a little better than their comrades to the south. The 2/RDF had one company scattered in and around Zebra and Zak Posts, lying between the Lempire-Vendhuile road and Lempire Road. Another platoon manned Rose Trench; this connected the two roads a little further to the west. Two other companies were in Ridge Reserve South, which protected against enemy approaches up St Patrick's Valley, while the other company was split between Enfer Wood, on the battalion's left flank, and a trench near Quid Copse. This position also sheltered the counter-attack platoons. HQ, housed in Sandbag Alley on the eastern edge of Lempire, was soon under attack. Little was heard from A Company to the front and north, but with the enemy pressing on through Sart Farm and Lempire East, the survivors fell back on Ridge Reserve. Their sister battalion, the 1/RDF, held the line between May Copse and Malassise Farm road. Battalion orders instructed the front line to be 'held at all costs' and that X and Z Companies in the Red Line would

(See map page 86)

(See map page 94)

Two Australian sergeants converse with members of a US machine-gun company which has its HQ installed in the shelters of Duncan Post. 28 September 1918. IWM E3392

'hold on to the last'.[4] The enemy was into the left of the Battle Zone by 10.45am and, by 12.50pm, a runner from May Copse delivered a message from Lieutenant Letchworth (OC Y Coy) that they were surrounded but would fight on. Contact was lost with the 2/RDF, who were seen withdrawing through Ronssoy, while on the left, Z Company, and any troops who had attached themselves to it, was ordered to withdraw to the railway embankment south-east of the Ste Emilie-Malassise road. This manoeuvre was designed to protect the right flank of the Munsters. About 70 men took up this new position.

With its main battle position in Ridge Reserve North, the 2/Munster, on the left of 48 Brigade, held the line between Epéhy and Malassise Farm. This trench ran from the strategically important high ground of Malassise Farm down the slope to Tetard Wood in Catelet Valley. The outposts were rapidly enveloped and, at 10.30am, when Lieutenant-Colonel Ireland attempted a reconnaissance to discover what was going on, the CO was mortally wounded. The redoubt at Malassise Farm fell at about 11.00am. Its defence was gallantly led by Lieutenant Kidd, but the position was out-flanked by the enemy advancing through the 1/RDF's line in Old Copse. One company was ordered to counter-attack the farm but it never received the message and the main fighting switched to Ridge Reserve North and Tetard Wood. When the mist cleared, the enemy was seen en masse in Catelet Valley. Lieutenant Whelan and C Company in Tetard Wood, with the 7/Leicester to their right, brought a heavy fire to bear on the valley, while troops in Ridge Reserve prevented the enemy from bringing artillery up Deelish Valley. Even when the Germans brought up a trench mortar and entered the trench from the Malassise Farm end, the garrison fought on until 5.00pm.

It was clear however that, with the Germans in occupation of Ronssoy, time was running out. During the afternoon Captain Chandler was ordered to form a strong point with two platoons on the Epéhy side of Vaughan's Bank. Until it was pounded by trench-mortar fire and out-flanked from the right, this post prevented the Germans debouching from Malassise Farm. The remnant of the original three officers and 50 men withdrew to Epéhy and joined with the 8/Leicester. Lieutenant Whelan had also taken the survivors of C Company into Epéhy. This company had succeeded in bringing down one enemy plane with Lewis gun fire and another by a single rifle shot which killed the pilot. Although wounded, Whelan continued his resistance until the following day when, having fired his last round and thrown his last bomb, he surrendered. When the battalion assembled at Tincourt on 22

March its trench strength had been reduced from 629 to 290. Among the unit's dead was Lieutenant Eynaud, attached from the King's Own Malta Regiment.

Despite the exceptionally heavy casualties and the loss of the front positions, on the first day the Germans had not completely penetrated or broken the 16th's Battle Zone. The division had been severely mauled and was relieved on 22 March by the 39th Division. Huge numbers had been captured but the same story had been repeated up and down the line of Fifth Army. Perhaps Haig was being a little too selective when he commented later that 'certain Irish units did very badly and gave way immediately the enemy showed'.[5]

September 1918

The recapture of the two villages in September 1918 was part of what the Battles Nomenclature Committee later called the Battle of Epéhy. On 18 September, one of the bloodiest days of the whole war, 36 Brigade of the 12th Division was in the Malassise Farm area. In heavy rain the 7/Sussex and 9/RF worked their way through a gas and HE bombardment from west of the two railways which ran across the basin, and took Ridge Reserve. The Fusiliers reached the outskirts of

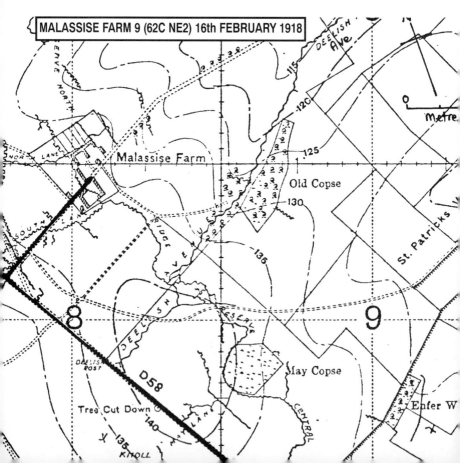

MALASSISE FARM 9 (62C NE2) 16th FEBRUARY 1918

the farm, but as the enemy refused to concede the ruins, patrols worked along Deelish Trench and established a post in Old Copse. At about 11.00am on the following day, the 6/Buffs of 37 Brigade pushed through and took the rest of Old Copse. The 6/Queen's experienced great difficulty in getting through the wire surrounding Malassise Farm, but eventually forced its way through and established posts about 500m further east.

The 18th Division wanted to avoid crossing the basin which lies between Ste Emilie and Ronssoy and so decided the thrust of its attack should come from the higher ground to the south and west. The divisional RE had built a series of dummy tanks, there being few real ones immediately available, but as visibility was so bad on the morning of 18 September, they never drew fire. When 54 Brigade attacked, fog shielded its movements, which was just as well as those tanks allocated to the brigade arrived late. The 7/West Kent went forward, supported by the 2/Beds who kept direction by following the trampled grass of their predecessors. The Kents forced their way into the southern part of Ronssoy and the Bedfords crossed Hussar Road. The northern portion of Ronssoy had been partially cleared by the 24/Welch of the 74th Division, but word came through that the 12th Division was being held up in Epéhy. The 11/RF pushed on northwards through Bassè Boulogne and Corporal Lewis of the 6/Northants won the VC for attacking two machine gun positions in Ronssoy. General Wood, GOC 55 Brigade entered Ronssoy armed with a cigar and his customary lance. He first captured a group of seven Germans and then took another 22 by the expedient of throwing chalk and an old boot down the steps of their dugout. By 11.00am the 6/Northants had cleared the northern portion of Ronssoy Road and had gained a substantial footing in Bassè Boulogne. The trenches around Quid Copse, which lay some 500m short of the objective, were cleared and two tanks came up later to help clear the rest of Bassè Boulogne. Keeping in touch with the Fusiliers on their right, the Northants established a line between Quid Post and Ridge Reserve.

By 5.00pm all of Ronssoy had been cleared and, under a creeping barrage, 55 Brigade advanced east towards Lempire, Yak and Zebra Posts. The enemy could be seen to be rapidly reinforcing his positions around the posts and intense fire was coming from X, Y and Z Copses. The fire was so fierce that the battalions withdrew to cover behind Bellicourt Road. The German defenders were troops of the *2nd Guards* and *232nd Divisions*, reinforced by men of the *121st Division*. Dawn's misty light saw patrols of the Northants advancing into May Copse, but

55 Brigade found to its cost that the X, Y and Z copses were still occupied. The Prussian Guards in Lempire and its surrounds appeared determined to slow for as long as possible the British advance towards the Hindenburg outpost lines.

At 11.00am on 19 September troops of 53 Brigade once more attempted to drive the Germans from the ruins of Lempire. The northern portion of the village was cleared and a line facing east was established running through Yak, Zebra and Grafton Posts. Any attempt to advance eastwards across the fields lying to the south of the village was prevented by fire coming from the three copses and from the machine-gun nests below the Lempire-Vendhuile road. The right flank of the 8/Berkshire, for example, was cut to pieces by fire from Doleful and Egg (also known as Ego) Posts, but the remainder of the battalion struggled through the village and successfully occupied Enfer Wood. At 2.00pm the West Kents jumped forward to a line Lempire Post–Yak Post–St Patrick's Lane, and Zebra Post was taken during the night. Soon after dawn on 20 September the three troublesome copses had also fallen to the 7/Queen's and 7/Buffs, while the 8/East Surrey took Queuchettes Wood. The 74th Division on their right had been badly held up by a German strong point known as the Quadrilateral on its extreme left. This was the former British position of Duncan Post. The 25/RoyalWelch Fusiliers and four tanks were ordered to storm it. The tanks failed to arrive but the attack went in, followed by another conducted by the 24/Welch. Both battalions gained little ground and were badly cut up for their pains. Eventually the 10/Shropshire, in conjunction with the 2/Bedford, captured the position and took 30 German machine guns as trophies.

The obstinate resistance of the *2nd Guards, 232nd* and *121st Divisions* and the *Alpine Corps* since 18 September, demonstrated the German intention of holding Templeux-le-Guérard, Ronssoy and Lempire as bastions to the Hindenburg Line. When they abandoned the three copses, the enemy was declaring that the final defence of the Hindenburg outpost system would rest on the Knoll and Gillemont Farm.

Notes

1. War Diary of 2/Royal Irish Regiment. Report dated 7 April 1918. WO.95.1979
2. M.Middlebrook, *The Kaiser's Battle*, p.120
3. War Diary of 11/Hants, 22 March 1918. WO.95.1966
4. War Diary of 1/Royal Dublin Fusiliers. Defence scheme. WO.95.1974
5. Middlebrook, op.cit, Chapter 13, has a lengthy discussion on how Fifth Army's 'collapse' of 21 March has since been viewed.

Ronssoy and Lempire today.

These two villages spread either side of the D58. Ronssoy lies to the west and Lempire to the east. Like most villages in the area, Ronssoy is a linear development but it does have another collection of houses which spread around a crescent to rejoin the main road near the rather interesting church. Clustered along the main road are some well-maintained houses and the *salle des fêtes*. The site of the former (See map page 100) *raperie* at the western end of the village has been landscaped. **(1)** Crops now grow on the site, overlooked by the inevitable crucifix. The communal **(2)** cemetery is east of the church.

Opposite the junction of the D6, an ungainly British concrete OP sits obtrusively in the garden of house No.2. **(3)** The former hamlets of Bassè Boulogne and La Paurelle are now indistinguishable from Ronssoy. The northern end of the village finishes abruptly immediately before a track leaves the road and heads off north of the wood. Another lane leaves the D58 between a row of houses 300m north of the junction with the D6 and winds down to the wood. Opposite this junction, a small lane loops round to join the D28 200m from its junction with the D58. This lane affords excellent views down St Patrick's Valley **(5)** and winds past a small and rather eccentric civilian cemetery. The entrance to a British HQ dugout can be seen immediately behind the wire fence on the south side of the cemetery. A ruined house stands at the junction of what the troops called Lempire Road and the lane. Lempire Road was one of the principal routes for relieving troops and ration parties on their way to the front posts in 1917.

A British observation post in Lempire, one of several which can still be seen in the area.

Lempire village is rather dilapidated. An unattractive church stands in front of a small communal cemetery and a small abandoned chapel squats unhappily opposite. The sad-looking houses immediately east of the church are on the site of Lempire West defences. 400m on from the church, the *Ruelle du Bois* leads off south towards X and Y Copses. **(6)** Z Copse no longer exists and X Copse is currently used as a dump for discarded farming implements. Colleen Post lay 400m west of Y Copse. Thistle Trench connected this post with Lempire East defences, having run to the south of the gardens of the houses lining the main road. These messuages formed Lempire Central defences. Another track coming in from the south leads down to a clump of trees growing on the site of Sart Farm. **(7)** Just after this track, the grey, neglected house (No.6) is on the site of the stronghold known as Lempire East. The bank running parallel 150 yards north of the road follows the line of Sandbag Alley. This trench housed battalion HQ for those units manning the sub-sector. In the fields beyond the bank were Yak and Zebra Posts. About 800m on from Lempire East is Unicorn Cemetery. **(8)**

Immediately after the motorway a track comes in from the north. It disappears into the motorway embankment after a few dozen yards but originally led up past Grafton Post to Little Priel Farm. Opposite is the new emergency exit from the motorway. The house a little further east is the rebuilt Tombois Farm. **(9)** It is a few score yards closer to Vendhuile than its predecessor and now occupies the site of Fleeceall Post. The motorway exit also doubles as a service road for a radio mast higher up the ridge. Its current route overlies part of both London Road and Fleet Street, passing the former sites of Egg and Doleful Posts on the way. The lane joins Gillemont Road 130m west of the motorway. Duncan Post is now under the western embankment of the motorway and the track which used to connect it with the three copses no longer exists. Queuchettes Wood to the south of Gillemont Road is clearly seen in the fields to the south-west. **(10)**

Malassise Farm **(14)** is now a thriving and extensive collection of farm buildings. Sitting behind a huge courtyard, the central farmhouse is a particularly splendid affair. The entrance comprises a large turreted dovecote with a date stone of 1632-1923. The overall pleasant aspect of the hamlet is marginally spoilt by probably the ugliest concrete silo ever designed. The road through the hamlet continues down Deelish Valley but leads only to fields.

The track of a light railway which came across the basin from Ste Emilie crossed the D58 100 yards north of the junction with *Rue*

Malassise Farm. It is now a thriving settlement sitting attractively among its surrounding fields of beet and wheat.

The railway embankment between Malassise Farm and Ste Emilie. One company of the 1/RDF held out here for a time after the farm had fallen.

Malassise. The railway curved round to run on top of Vaughan's Bank before it joined with the broad gauge south of Epéhy station. This line was later converted to standard gauge and remains in occasional use. At the junction of the farm's access road with the D58 is the memorial to the 12th Division. **(13)** Modified in recent years, this memorial was identical to the division's other one at Feuchy near Arras. It lists the division's battle honours on each of its six sides. The final face simply has 'Victory'. Quid Copse **(15)**, Enfer Wood **(16)**, May Copse **(17)** and Old Copse **(18)** have all regrown, although May Copse is now more a collection of bushes and trees rather than a bona fide wood.

Tour of Ronssoy and Lempire
(Tour Map 4)
9kms, 5.6miles. 2 hours

Park at the *salle des fêtes* in Ronssoy and walk down to the communal cemetery. **(2)** This lies towards the eastern end of the village, south of the main road. Walk back up to the main road and turn right to the junction with the D58. A British observation post can be seen in the yard of the house immediately opposite the junction. **(3)** Turn left and right towards Lempire at the CWGC sign to Unicorn Cemetery. Call in at the churchyard **(4)** and continue along the D28

The rather sparse collection of trees which now constitutes May Copse. This, and Old Copse beyond, were defended by the 1/RDF on 21 March. A long trench, known in this sector as Ridge Reserve Central, came down the slope towards the camera.

through the village. X and Y Copses **(6)** can be reached by the *Ruelle du Bois* on the right. Unicorn Cemetery is immediately west of the motorway. **(8)**

Go under the motorway and pass Tombois Farm on the right. **(9)** Take the track on the left which follows the bottom of Tombois Valley to the Quarries. At the crossroads in front of the Quarries, **(11)** turn left and climb up to Little Priel Farm. **(12)** Drop down to the site of Catelet Copse and pass under the motorway. Turn left and follow this track (Lempire Road) for about 1800m. At the T-junction by the ruined house, turn right to pass the civilian cemetery. **(5)** Follow this minor road until it becomes a grass track and joins the D58. Turn left and then right at the main junction to return to the car.

Drive up towards Epéhy, passing Quid Copse **(15)** on the left. Turn right at the 12th Division's memorial **(13)** to go past Malassise Farm. **(14)** Turn around at the farm and return to the D58.

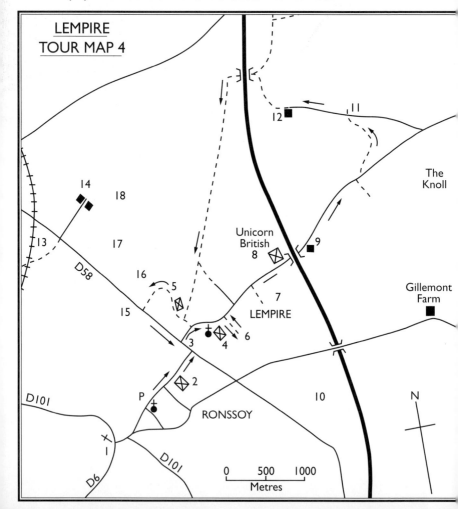

LEMPIRE
TOUR MAP 4

Chapter Six

GILLEMONT FARM AND THE KNOLL

Although unrecognised by most visitors to the Western Front, the few acres of land which constitute Gillemont Farm and the Knoll were some of the most heavily fought over of 1917 and 1918. Their present-day aura of tranquillity disguises the violence and bloodshed that the unhappy attackers and defenders endured between the severe snow, rain and cold of April 1917, and the equally damp but warmer days of September 1918.

Elements of the BEF's 3rd Division might have noticed the collection of farm buildings and the crop-laden crest to its north as they passed through the area on 27 August 1914. To these survivors of Le Cateau, the farm would have appeared identical to a hundred

Conditions endured by troops in early spring of April 1917.

others they had passed during the Retreat. The war moved on and the hummock of the Knoll and the nearby buildings saw no hostile action until the German withdrawal. Following on the heels of the Germans, in April 1917 the 5th Cavalry Division and the 48th Division occupied the ground in front of the two features and came to a halt. The German outpost line stretched across their front which now lay in a valley to the west of the ridge of which the Knoll and the farm form the highest parts. The first of what would develop into a succession of extremely violent battles for the possession of this ridge soon followed.

The first real attempt against both features was made by 145 **Spring** Brigade, with the 4/Ox & Bucks temporarily attached. The original **1917** plan for a night attack was abandoned in favour of a day light effort supported by a Field Company of RE and the 5/Sussex (Pioneers). Heavy machine-gun fire from enemy troops sited in pits in front of the farm tore into the Ox & Bucks when D Company crested the ridge. Platoons temporarily lost touch with each other and with the sure knowledge that the farm was strongly wired and held, the attackers, with at least ten dead and nearly 50 wounded, were ordered to withdraw. Five days later another attempt was made. On this occasion the 8/Worcester was to go for the farm while the 6/Gloucester went for the Knoll. Two companies of the Worcesters made a pre-dawn assault on the farm and took it, but another company, which was attacking Quennet Copse across the valley, was held up by wire. Meanwhile the Gloucesters had failed to take the Knoll. When dawn broke, the two companies in the farm endured a storm of fire from the Knoll to the east and Malakoff Wood to the south-east. The fire became so overwhelming that the Worcesters were forced to give ground. They fought their way back to the original start line. Nine officers and nearly 160 other ranks were killed or wounded. Another effort was made later in the day (24 April). This time the 7/Worcester was to attack the farm, the 4/Gloucester the Knoll and the 4/Berkshire, Quennet Copse. Once again the Worcesters forced their way into the farm and hastily entrenched. As dawn spread from the eastern skies, like their comrades in the other battalions, the Worcesters came under fire from three directions. The flanks had failed, and the Worcesters had to abandon the captured trenches to the east of the farm and consolidate the rapidly deteriorating ruins of the farmyard. Having lost about 150 men, the battalion was later relieved. Although the Knoll and Quennet Copse remained in enemy hands, the farm was occupied. The position provided good observation down Claymore and Macquincourt Valleys but the British hold on it was extremely tenuous.

Soon after the 42nd Division, recently arrived from Egypt, relieved the 48th, the Germans recaptured the farm. This apparently led to some free-for-all fights between the Midlanders and the Lancastrians in sunken lanes to the rear.[1] The former accused the latter of being 'windy' and of not putting up sufficient resistance to the enemy attacks. The 5/Warwick managed to recaptured the bulk of the farm buildings, but the Knoll remained in German hands. In mid-May, the Cavalry Corps took over the sector. The dismounted troopers continued to entrench the farm, enduring on many occasions deluges of gas and torrents of high explosive. On 10 June the Scots Greys raided the enemy positions east of the farm with 'great success',[2] but the German retaliation which followed cost the Greys and 10/Hussars over a dozen killed. Later in the month, the Germans launched a determined attack on the British trenches in the farm. After a prolonged and bitter battle, the enemy were eventually ejected. It was during a similar enemy attack in May that the MP for South Oxfordshire, Valentine Fleming

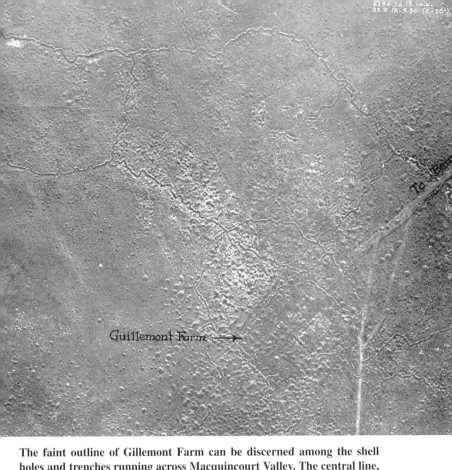

628A.7d.13.14.a.
23.9 18.5.30 (E.26')

Guillemont Farm ⟶

To Banteux

The faint outline of Gillemont Farm can be discerned among the shell holes and trenches running across Macquincourt Valley. The central line, running right-left, is Willow Trench. Grub Lane connects it with Lone Tree Trench. Ely Way, running just north of the road, connects Willow Trench with Gillemont Crescent, a continuation of Lone Tree Trench.

Trees now surround a peaceful Gillemont Farm. This photograph shows the area occupied by British forces from April 1917. To the rear of the farm and on either side, the land falls away sharply.

DSO was killed. Fleming served in the Oxfordshire Hussars and its unit history gives what must rate as one of the longest regimental eulogies written for a man who was never its commanding officer. Although the account contains the usual terms of praise and remembrance, Fleming was clearly considered to be something special:

> *No greater blow could have befallen the Regiment than the death of Major Fleming. Beloved by his many friends, worshipped by his squadron, admired and respected by all, he was a most gallant officer, a born leader of men...he was able to control men freely by strength of character and personal example rather than by force of military discipline...[He could have] with perfect justification have obtained a responsible staff appointment and no one would have thought the worse of him...The Regiment lost in Val Fleming not only a brave and capable officer but also a character of singular charm and attraction...the staunchest and truest of friends, the gayest and brightest of comrades...the athletic figure with the long, quick stride and the keen eager face, the laughter and talk full of shrewd thrusts which enlivened good days and bad, merry evenings in billets, wet and anxious nights in trenches. He left a gap that could not be filled, a memory that could not be forgotten.*[3]

Fleming was undertaking a reconnaissance with Lieutenant Francis Silvertop when a German bombardment came down on the farm. The regimental history notes that it was:

> *'a strange irony of fate that, having left the Regiment in September 1915 to join the infinitely more dangerous service of the RFC, he had returned to us unscathed, only to fall in a chance raid on an isolated post'.*[4]

Both men were originally buried in Ste Emilie Chateau Cemetery, but they now lie together in Templeux-le-Guérard British.

In July the 35th Division relieved the cavalry and decided that it should attempt an attack on both the Knoll and the eastern end of the farm spur. When corps heavy and field artillery units were promised to the division, the scheme was expanded from its original concept of a raid into a full-blown assault. The 18/HLI of 106 Brigade and the 15/Cheshire and 15/Sherwood Foresters of 105 Brigade practised the assault on replica trenches constructed in the rear. An enemy raid on the trenches of the 17/Royal Scots in front of Gillemont Farm on 6 August was repulsed, but it was noted that the enemy was actively strengthening his wire on the Knoll. Preparations continued. More artillery moved into Ronssoy Wood, assembly trenches were dug and battle HQ constructed and connected with telephone cables to Brigade and Division. Elements of the 4th Cavalry Division returned to the sector to relieve troops opposite the Knoll. These passed to the rear and joined the other battalions to rehearse the coming attack. As he observed the infantry marching back from the line, one of the cavalry's senior officers noted that 'we should have taken the Knoll when we were in the line'.[5]

On 18 August the bombardment opened on the enemy wire and rear positions. The impressive fire of corps and divisional guns was supplemented by a 9.45-inch trench mortar firing from Tombois Farm. The 15/Cheshire and 15/SF followed the barrage and within 15 minutes the Knoll had been taken. If sufficient troops had been available, the enemy trench running down the hill to the Lempire-Vendhuile road could also have been captured. Casualties among the two assaulting battalions amounted to fewer than 50 killed and a little over 100 wounded. Two communication trenches running back to the battle HQ were rapidly dug and wired by the Pioneers, and a new front trench was taped and excavated by forward troops. German counter-attacks began almost immediately. During the course of the following two days, the battle raged to and fro. The fighting was savage and almost incessant. Second Lieutenant Hardy Parsons of the 14/Gloucester was awarded a posthumous VC for single-handedly halting the enemy at one of the advanced posts on the Knoll's southern flank. Burned by flammenwerfer fire the young subaltern later died of his wounds.

The attack on Gillemont Farm had begun badly for the 18/HLI

The grave of Second Lieutenant Parsons in Villers-Faucon Communal Cemetery. Parsons, of the 14/Gloucester, won his VC for outstanding bravery at the Knoll in August 1917.

105

when a preventative barrage crashed down on its assembly positions. Some reorganisation of the companies was required but, when the British barrage began, the battalion stormed over and fought its way into the enemy lines. The trenches were heavily garrisoned and ferocious hand-to-hand fighting ensued. Despite this, a later report claimed that not one of the HLI was wounded or killed by the German garrison. The enemy fled.Within minutes the captured positions were linked to battalion HQ and with the arrival of parties from the 203rd Field Company and the 19/NF, consolidation began. A few minor German counter-attacks were driven off, but a more persistent effort was made during the morning of 20 August. This was broken up when the SOS brought down a decisive bombardment on both the German first and second waves.

When the 18/HLI was relieved by the 19/DLI on the night of 20-21 August, it had sustained only 25 killed and 90 wounded. Four nights later it returned to the trenches which cut and snaked their way through the devastated farm courtyard, paddock and buildings. At 4.15am a bombardment, so intense that within minutes the entire front line was obliterated and the Lewis gun posts destroyed, fell upon the recent arrivals. As enemy bombers worked down the front positions from the north, the HLI was forced to withdraw. A counter-attack from Doleful Post withered away when it was caught in the open by the German barrage. Attempts to bomb up the communication trenches were frustrated by heavy knife rests, a resolute enemy and the fact that the Germans could throw their stick grenades 20m further than most of the HLI could hurl their Mills. The survivors clung on to what had been the support trench of 20 August and decided that nothing but an organised attack with sufficient artillery preparation would regain the lost ground.

The 19/DLI was called up from Lempire and, at about 7.30pm, three under strength companies moved up from Duncan Lane and eventually regained the old front line. Some resistance in the Blunt Nose was overcome and several German counter-attacks, one down Willow Trench from the north and another from the southern part of Gillemont Trench, were repulsed. The DLI even managed to recapture two Lewis guns and three Stokes mortars lost by the HLI and the TMB. With the two foes glaring at each other across a No Man's Land of about 30m in width, the line, for the time being, stabilised. Lieutenant-Colonel Lawrenson of the 18/HLI reported:

'We seem to have inflicted heavy casualties on the enemy and it appears that...at one time [he] had been driven back, but came

on again when reinforced and when most of our garrison had ceased to exist'.

He concluded:

'I very much regret that the battalion should have lost a position so recently taken by them, but they did not do so without having put up a splendid fight and having accounted for so many of the enemy'.[6]

The enemy was reasonably content with the position as it stood at Gillemont Farm. However, he was considerably uneasy about the observation over the Vendhuile canal crossings which occupation of the Knoll gave to the British. Consequently, on 30 August the Germans began a severe bombardment of the Knoll and battery positions to the rear. Early next morning, assisted by mist, a dense smoke-screen and a very intense bombardment by artillery and trench mortars, the enemy swarmed onto the crest and ejected the 17/West Yorks. A counter-attack up Cochran Avenue reached to within 80m of the top, but the company was forced to withdraw to the blocks established in Crellin and Cochran Avenues near to the sunken lane. During the brief hurricane bombardment and the subsequent infantry attack, the West Yorks had suffered nearly 50 killed.

The short occupation of the two features had allowed the British time to observe and sketch more of the Hindenburg Line; this information was used to supplement detail gleaned from aerial

German shock-troops preparing to storm a position.

photographs. From its positions west of the farm, the 35th Division could see down Macquincourt Valley almost to the canal. However, the trenches which permitted this view remained themselves under observation from the Knoll and the farm. An uneasy and frequently punctuated calm descended upon the two features for the next few months. Patrols crawled about in No Man's Land and bombardments came down on those front positions which were far enough apart to prevent inflicting casualties on their own side. On 18 November a 200-strong German raiding party attacked the line at Gillemont held by the 4/Loyal North Lancs. The enemy bombed down the communication trench leading to Duncan Post, killing and wounding most of the garrison. HQ details held up the bombers, who were then forced back by a counter-attack sent up Ken Lane. A heavy bombardment was put down on Duncan and Doleful Posts while the enemy withdrew. The Loyals lost 13 killed, 21 wounded and 48 missing.

November 1917

As part of the diversionary scheme for the Battle of Cambrai the 4/Royal Lancashire made a limited assault on the farm. Although initially successful, the attackers were soon driven back; an attempt on the Knoll was even more unsuccessful because the wire had been hardly touched by the preparatory bombardment. The German counter-stroke passed a little to the north of the farm and so apart from some fairly ferocious shelling, its garrison of the 7/King's remained unmolested. When Cambrai was closed down, the main British positions remained some way west of the two features. The westernmost area of the farm remained occupied as a forward post, constituting in March 1918 part of the 16th Division's defences. General Gough's insistence that the Forward Zone of the Irish division should be heavily garrisoned meant that, on 21 March, the farm was manned by two platoons of the 7/Royal Irish Regiment. They, and their comrades in nearby Duncan and Cat Posts, were rapidly enveloped by the German penetration.

March 1917

In September 1918, having resolutely slogged its way through Ronssoy and Lempire, the 18th Division captured the enemy redoubts created in the former British Forward Zone. Maintaining its reputation as one of the best divisions in the BEF, the 18th had traversed and conquered much ground, suffering very heavily in the process. With companies averaging about 70 rifles, the division's battalions anticipated a well-earned respite. Their reward, however, was to be sent in again with the task of clearing the ferociously defended outposts of the Hindenburg Line. Once they had been taken, fresh divisions would be brought up to break the line itself.

September 1918

Typical of the defences which faced the assaulting troops of September 1918, these belts of wire were a little to the south of Gillemont Farm.

On 21 September 53 Brigade, assisted by seven tanks, was detailed to take the Knoll. 54 Brigade was allocated the trenches lying across the top of Macquincourt Valley between the Knoll and the farm, while 231 Brigade of the 74th Division was to attack the farm itself. Zero was 5.40am. The 7/West Kent took Sart Farm, a nasty stronghold bristling with trench mortars and machine guns, while on its left the 10/Essex passed through Tombois Farm. The Essex were then brought to a halt by a curtain of fire coming from the front and both flanks. Enemy machine guns on Gillemont Farm spur, Grafton Post and in Lark Trench poured an unremitting fire into one company, while another was forced back from Egg Post. Further south, as the 7/Bedford approached Doleful and Duncan Posts, one company of the 6/Northants progressed as far as Island Traverse. The attack in all areas petered out in the face of resolute resistance. Under a canopy of stars and a bright moon, the two brigades tried again at 12.15am. Some progress was made towards Duncan and Doleful Posts but, as it was uneven, the Germans managed to infiltrate between the advancing platoons. During the afternoon a strong counter-attack south of Tombois Farm was repulsed and a party of 44 men of the 2/Bedfords seized 150 prisoners from Doleful and Duncan Posts. Later German counter-attacks against the two posts were contained, although the enemy did maintain his grip on Egg Post for a further two days. During the night of 24-25 September, II (US) Corps arrived to take over the line in preparation for its assault on the Hindenburg Line.

The capture of these small but significant posts was described as 'some of the hardest-won ground in the history of the division'.[7] It was during these attacks that Lance-Corporal Lewis of the 6/Northants, who had won a VC for his courage at Ronssoy only three days earlier, was killed. Unfortunately, despite the gruelling slog across the rolling hills and valleys, the 18th and 74th Divisions' objectives had not been secured. The Knoll and Gillemont Farm remained in German hands. Helped by the exhausted brigades of the 18th Division, the next

Australian troops and stretcher bearers in support to the 27th (US) Division move up a communication trench towards Gillemont Farm on 29 September 1918.

attempt on the two positions was to be made by the American 27th and 30th Divisions. It is more convenient to deal with these final attacks as part of the larger late-September assault on the Hindenburg Line. The fall of the Knoll and the eventual capture of the farm are therefore covered in the chapter on Bellicourt. For now, the final words on the farm can best perhaps be left with the historian of the Oxford Hussars. After the war he thought:

> Gillemont Farm has always been remembered with special interest by those of the Regiment who were there. For them it is almost the chief landmark in the middle years of the war. The fighting was little more than an affair of outposts; the place a tiny pin-point in the Allied line, not marked on any but the largest maps. The farm was an isolated post, rather important in this particular sector; little outside support could be hoped for and any squadron holding it knew it must rely entirely on its own grit and resolution to resist an attack. The casualties, the sharp and sudden raids, the comparative novelty and independence of the situation, all combined to stamp it on men's memories, so that they came to associate the Regiment with the place in a way one never did with an ordinary piece of trench line.[8]

Notes

1. E.Vaughan, *Some Desperate Glory*, p.91. Vaughan is particularly critical of the 10/Manchester, the Oldham Territorials. One company of the battalion did occupy and hold the farm in May. Its War Diary makes no mention of the alleged behind the lines incidents. Vaughan's chronology and accuracy are, at times, suspect.
2. A.Horne, op.cit. 10 June 1917
3. A.Keith-Falconer, *The Oxfordshire Hussars in the Great War*, p.206-7
4. Ibid
5. Horne, op.cit. 6 August 1917.
6. War Diary of 18/Highland Light Infantry. WO.95.2490
7. G.Nichols, *The 18th Division in the Great War*, p.413
8. Keith-Falconer, op.cit. p.219.

A working party about to begin clearing and salvaging amid the wire defences of the Hindenburg Line.

Gillemont Farm and the Knoll today.

The Knoll has once again reverted to arable land. Yearly harvests of beet and wheat grow where once nothing but poisoned, blood-soaked ground offered meagre protection to frightened men. Gillemont Farm was rebuilt in the 1920s. Now a well-proportioned and substantial farmhouse, it stands sentinel over Claymore Valley from behind a screen of conifers. Window boxes and flower tubs in the courtyard provide a riot of summer colour. Some of the outbuildings are not quite so attractive, but it is a working farm.

The grass paddock on its western side fills an area which marked the usual limit of British tenancy. The German front line trenches ran across the road's dog-leg: Willow Trench ran into Macquincourt Valley to the north; Claymore Trench fell away towards what is now the American cemetery to the south. 180m to the east on the reverse slopes, lay the support trench, Gillemont Crescent. A new gravel track heads south from Gillemont Road down the western end of Claymore Valley almost to Quennet Copse. The several sunken lanes north of Gillemont Road which led towards the Knoll are now under the plough. Cochran Avenue, Island Traverse and the other posts and trenches held by the British in 1917, now lie beneath the crops. The only evidence today of the violence which consumed the area are the lumps of rusted shrapnel and unexploded shells concealed within the corrugated earth.

Macquincourt Valley, with the almost indiscernible Knoll in front of the clump of trees left of centre. The area in front of the camera was riven by trenches and was rarely quiet until British, Australian and US forces reached the canal at the foot of the valley in September 1918.

THE KNOLL

MACQUINCOURT VALLEY

Tour of Gillemont Farm and the Knoll
(Tour Map 5)
7.1kms, 4.4miles. 1.25 hours

Park at Vendhuile church. Climb up the slope of the Lempire road. As the slope steepens and the end of the village approaches, turn left onto the *Rue Delattre*. Follow for about 200m until a junction with a shrine on the right. Face the shrine and take the small tarmac road on the left. The road soon degenerates into gravel. After 1200m turn right

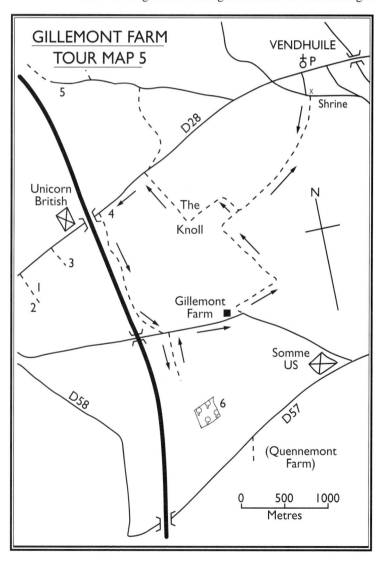

GILLEMONT FARM
TOUR MAP 5

VENDHUILE

P

5

Shrine

D28

Unicorn
British

N

4

The

Knoll

3

1

2

Gillemont
Farm

Somme
US

D58

6

D57

(Quennemont
Farm)

0   500   1000
Metres

onto another gravel track. This bends to the left after 200m and climbs up onto the Knoll. Standing on the crest, the visitor can easily appreciate the importance of the position. Panoramic views of Bony, Gillemont Farm, X and Y Copses **(1 & 2)**, Sart Farm **(3)**, Little Priel Farm **(5)**, Lempire and Epéhy can all be enjoyed. Walk over the crest and take a 90-degree right turn to follow the track down to the D28.

Turn left onto the D28 and walk past Fleeceall Post and Tombois Farm. **(4)** Turn left onto the service road of the motorway. Follow the track up past the mast and take in the good views down Macquincourt Valley and across to Gillemont Farm. Doleful Post is under the motorway just west of the mast. The track joins Gillemont Road. Turn left. 100m on the right a gravel track leads down towards Quennet Copse. **(6)** Wigan Way crossed this track after 300m. There is no

Gillemont Farm still yields its 'iron harvest'. This shell was unearthed by the plough in the autumn of 1997.

southern exit from the lane but it provides good views down Claymore Valley. Return to Gillemont Road, turn right and walk along to the farm.

Turn left as if going into the farmyard immediately before the road does a dog-leg. Turn right before going through the farm gates, pass across the edge of the outbuildings and pick up a line of telegraph poles. This lane crosses the path of Willow Trench. It turns 90 degrees left and drops down into Macquincourt Valley. It then climbs and rejoins the track you left to go across to the Knoll. Keep straight on and return to the shrine.

114

Chapter Seven

BELLICOURT AND BONY

The American II Corps (27th and 30th Divisions) moved into the area in front of Gillemont Farm on 24-25 September. The units were allowed two days to observe and familiarise themselves with the sector before launching an attack against the farm and the Knoll.

The canal tunnel under Bellicourt and Bony runs for a length of 3.57 miles. It was opened in 1810 and for most of its length is unlined. The Germans made the tunnel into an integral part of the Hindenburg defences and, at between 100 and 130 feet below the surface, it made an ideal shell-proof shelter for troops and administration. Billeting barges for soldiers of the local defences filled the first 1100m of the southern end. Continuous board platforms linked the barges to the towpath which runs the entire length of the tunnel. The waterway is over 21 feet wide, with the towpath adding another 4'6" to the width of the tunnel. Depth of water varies but through most of the length is today about 8'. In 1918 the water level was 7' lower at the northern end than at the southern.

The Germans constructed concrete barrier walls just inside both portals; access into the tunnel was through a door built on the towpath.

Inexperienced in the ways of war and of the French language, US troops are taught the essentials of how to obtain bread and give a challenge when on sentry duty.

The southern entrance of the canal tunnel in October 1918. Shattered trees line the bank and a wooden screen just inside the entrance shielded a concrete dam 30m further in.

The barriers and certainly the southern portal had machine-gun slits built into them. There are vertical air shafts about every 500m and a large number of water seepage channels. Several of these tunnels were mined in such a way that if blown by the defenders, the explosions would cause the main tunnel to collapse. By installing compressed pumps to power drills, German engineers had excavated large chambers off the tunnel. A light railway had even been run into the eastern side to carry out spoil and bring in supplies. Among other things, these chambers housed aid posts, battalion HQ and officers' billets. The tunnel was an ideal refuge but, as it suffered from continual water seepage through the walls, it was always damp and probably pretty unpleasant.

The tunnel's principal purpose was to protect the garrisons of the Hindenburg Line from Allied bombardments but, at the same time, allow a rapid and easy exit for the defenders to repel infantry assaults. Along its length there were over 30 access tunnels which ran up directly into the trenches above. Often over 100m in length and sometimes at an angle which required them to be stepped, on the surface these exits gave the appearance of being nothing more than a conventional dugout. They were so heavily disguised and camouflaged with screens and brushwood that British aircraft had failed to identify them. Although the Allies were ignorant of the actual number and location of the tunnels, it was acknowledged that when an attack on the main defences was attempted, strong guards would have to be posted at the tunnels' exits.

The route of the tunnel is easily identified. A mound of excavated spoil follows its line; the two main trenches of the Hindenburg Line ran to the west of this mound. About 1500m to the west of the front trenches was the outpost line, while roughly equidistant to the east was another formidable system of trenches known as Le Catelet-Nauroy Line. Enormous thought and experience had gone into the design and construction of the trench systems. Trenches in the Bellicourt area were cut through chalk and had only a minimal amount of revetting. Even in the most ferocious of bombardments, they could generally be relied upon to hold their shape well. They were up to 10 feet wide and

The concrete dam inside the southern end, with three machine-gun loop holes and a door allowing access along the tow path. IWM E3598

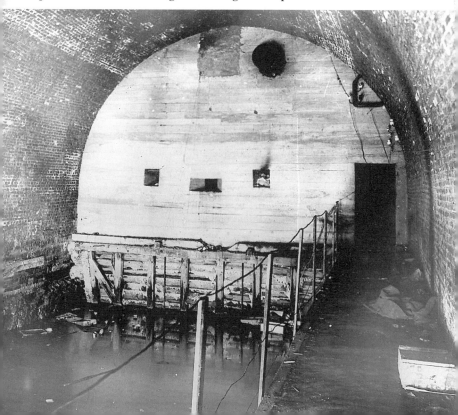

A typical trench of the Hindenburg system, near Bony. The dugout entrance on the left has been protected by a concrete lintel. IWM E3581

8 feet deep. In places there were six successive lines of trenches, with wire in-between. Beneath the trenches was an intricate system of dugouts. These were lined with mining timbers, often 30 feet deep and frequently lit by electricity. On the surface, well-sited and almost flush with the ground were the concrete machine-gun posts. Protected by belts of double apron or concertina wire, these emplacements were difficult to spot and difficult to overcome. To the rear of the forward positions were the more substantial concrete bunkers. These were the command posts, signalling stations and aid posts. Often connected to the forward trenches and to each other by tunnels, they presented any attacker with a bewildering choice of where they should bomb next.

It was against this supposedly impregnable line that the very inexperienced American II Corps was to be seriously blooded. Originally the task was allotted to the Australian Corps but its divisions were in such bad shape that additional help would be required. After their gruelling slog across the land east of Péronne, General Monash had promised his 1st and 4th Divisions a significant rest. Although still very under-strength, the 2nd, 3rd and 5th Divisions were considered to be again battleworthy. When Monash was offered the help of the two American divisions, currently training with British Second Army to the north, he leaped at the opportunity. American divisions were almost double the paper strength of British ones so Monash believed that provided the artillery could do its job of wire breaking, trench destruction and demoralisation, sheer weight of numbers would carry the Americans through. They were to be the spearhead, blasting their way through the defences, with the more battle hardened Australians following through and exploiting the breaches. Monash viewed the tunnel and its surrounding defences as a 'bridge': get across, consolidate and then expand the bridgehead.

Great emphasis was put on ensuring that, once the breach was made, the supporting troops could get through. The Australians had not

Troops of the 30th (US) Division head towards their assembly area on 29 September 1918. The tanks, Mark Vs of the British 8th Battalion, carry cribs to enable them to cross the deep trenches of the Hindenburg Line.

experienced the type of landscape which has become synonymous with the Great War since leaving Ypres in 1917. The area in front of Bellicourt and Bony, especially in the region between Quennemont and Cologne Farms, was very badly cut up. It was decided that 102nd and 105th Regiment of Engineers, assisted by the Pioneers of the Australian 3rd and 5th Divisions, would repair and extend four principal roads across the battlefield. These would be the principal arteries along which the supply of men and munitions would be maintained.

Crucial as this means of carrying supplies to the front was, it would come to nothing if the German defences remained intact. As Gillemont Farm and the Knoll remained in German hands, the Americans and Australians faced an additional hurdle. The attackers had not only to break the Hindenburg Line itself, but still had first to get through its outpost defences. At 5.30am on 27 September, the 27th Division launched an attack by three battalions of 106th Regiment and 12 tanks. They had to advance between 1000-1500m on a front of 4,000m. The troops forged forward and penetrated the outpost line. Some stormed on beyond, but reports arriving at the rear became increasingly confused. Success signals were apparently seen at the Knoll, only to be followed by messages from the British 12th Division that the position

Tanks which were accompanying the Americans on 29 September, blown up in the line of the old British wire. The uncovered mines, 'plum pudding' trench-mortar bombs, shown in the photograph, were originally sown beneath the wire.

was again lost. Although many Americans seem to have gone past Gillemont and Quennemont Farms, the two sites were definitely still in German hands. In their enthusiasm to get on, American troops failed to mop up the many trenches and dugouts over which they stormed. Once they were over, defenders emerged from their depths to fire into the flanks and backs of the attackers.

Gillemont Farm once again lived up to its evil reputation. Between March and September the site had been converted into what the Australians called a tank fort. These positions contained at least one field gun, several heavy and light machine guns, anti-tank rifles and at least a platoon of infantry. Countless British and German soldiers had already died within the bloody confines of the farm, and now their numbers were swollen by the addition of American soldiers. A German report on Americans captured at Gillemont and Quennemont Farms criticised them for lacking 'dash and morale'.[1] The Australian historian believes this was an unfair assessment. It was not low morale which foiled the Americans, but inexperience, a lack of officers and the difficulties inherent in attacking such a strong position. It simply 'asked too much of their training'.[2]

The problem General Monash faced in the evening of 27 September was what to do next. With most Americans back at their start line, Monash wanted a day's delay to give the artillery the chance of obliterating the enemy defences. Rawlinson insisted that as the assault was part of a far grander scheme, involving not only Fourth Army to the immediate south, the Americans and Australians would have to conform to the overall plan. To exacerbate further Monash's difficulties, a pilot's report suggested that there were still many groups of Americans in the German outpost line. This meant that he could not bring the bombardment down on these still formidable defences before the next assault. An unsatisfactory compromise was reached; the barrage would fall on the eastern side of the outpost line but 34 tanks would set off ten minutes before the infantry in order to capture the ground not taken on 27 September.

To the British 12th and 18th Divisions, this compromise was a recipe for disaster. These two divisions, both exhausted and very under-strength following their advance towards Epéhy and beyond, were detailed to assist the Americans. The 18th Division was to cooperate with the 27th's left flank and take the northern section of the Knoll. British staffs were appalled at the prospect of attacking without a barrage and devised a scheme of their own which, if it worked, would cover the approach to their objectives. At 5.40am on 29 September, the

British divisions moved off under cover of a particularly ferocious barrage; the Americans to their left advanced towards Gillemont Farm and the southern part of the Knoll without the benefit of shrieking steel pouring onto their defenders.

The 11/RF and 6/Northants of 54 Brigade kept Tombois Road on their left and climbed the Knoll. After heavy fighting, the Germans were finally evicted from Knoll Switch. However, attempts to push on down Macquincourt Valley were frustrated by the intensity of machine-gun fire coming from Gillemont Farm. Two battalions of 55 Brigade, which were supposed to be passing through and on into Vendhuile, remained around Fleeceall and Doleful Posts awaiting developments. German counter-attacks developed in Macquincourt Valley and the garrison of the Knoll was subjected to unrelenting artillery and machine-gun fire. Until the Americans could get forward, and there seemed little prospect of them doing so, the 18th Division could do nothing except hold on grimly to the battered crest.

The 27th US Division had suffered hugely at Gillemont Farm. Its men

> 'were magnificent, but their staffs were lacking in experience...[and their] communications... lamentable'.[3]

The Australian official historian thought:

> 'It is hard to believe that the 27th Division ever had a chance of success'.[4]

The advance against the farm was hampered by the lack of a barrage and by many of the supporting tanks either being knocked out by gunfire, getting themselves lost in the mist and smoke, or being blown up by old British 'mines'. Initially, there were reports that the attack was proceeding according to plan but, as the Australians moved forward, Americans were seen streaming back half a mile behind their former front line. Machine-gun bullets tore into the ranks of the 38th Battalion, and when the 39th and 40th Battalions crested the ridge south of the Knoll, they came under a withering fire from Gillemont Farm. Americans were pouring back up Macquincourt Valley, leaderless and with little idea of what they should be doing. So parlous was their state that the Australian official photographer forsook his camera and rallied some bewildered US infantry around Willow Trench. The 38th Battalion was held up in front of the farm and the 41st to its right was thwarted by fire coming from around Benjamin Post. Against a torrent of metal, a section of the 11th MG Company and troops of the 59th Battalion launched a desperate attack from the junction of five tracks on the Bony road and finally forced a way into Quennemont

Farm. Nine cars of the 17th Armoured Car Battalion and eight Whippets moved up to the 'Five Ways' before advancing down the slope towards Bony. Anti-tank fire from a German pill box on the ridge put paid to four cars and four tanks before the others prudently scuttled for safety.

Men of the 44th and 59th Battalions passed south of Malakoff Farm and pushed on towards Bellicourt. They found a number of Americans sheltering behind the canal mound and, with their help, reached the main road east of the tunnel. As the mist cleared, German carrying parties could be seen moving freely across Vauban Valley in the direction of Bony. To the Australians and their adopted Americans, it was clear that the US attack on Gillemont Farm and Bony had made little if no progress. To their south, in the 5th (Australian) and 30th (US) Divisions' sector, things had gone a little better. Troops of the 57th and 58th Battalions crossed Mount Olympus and descended into Bellicourt. Several hundred Americans were discovered sheltering behind the canal mound. These were easily persuaded to get going, passing the village to the north, while Australian 8 Brigade entered the settlement from the south and east. Its battalions had picked up a number of lost Americans around Quarry Wood; these troops also showed a great willingness to attach themselves to any unit which had officers prepared to tell them what to do.

Troops and transport poured into Bellicourt; while the mist stayed, they were relatively safe. As it began to clear, the packed roads provided a magnificent target for German gunners to the east. By this time, the Americans were supposed to have reached the German gun lines at Nauroy. Taking matters into its own hands, the 32nd Australian Battalion commandeered two tanks, rounded up a number of leader-less Americans and passed between Bellicourt and the tunnel mouth. Pill box garrisons either surrendered or were killed inside their concrete posts. The Australians surged on and reached Nauroy. Now, with their flanks in the air, they pushed south-east until they linked up with the 4/Leicester of the 46th Division near Billiard Copse. In this southern sector, an advance of about 4,000m had been achieved. Large numbers of guns and prisoners were taken and the attack had not yet lost its momentum. Unfortunately, further north, the Americans of the 27th Division and their Australian mentors were still in deep trouble.

Large numbers of the 108th Infantry Regiment were holed up in South Gillemont Trench and the isolated posts in Claymore Valley. Any sign of movement brought down fire from the farm and the main Hindenburg Line defences about Bony. Some Australians of the 38th and 39th Battalions joined them and attempted to get on. Without artillery support, their attempts did not achieve anything except to add to the already substantial casualty list. A few men did reach the junction of the Hargicourt and Gillemont Farm roads, where the knocked-out hulls of the eight armoured cars and Whippets provided some cover. As night fell the situation remained confused, but largely static. Next day, two Australian brigades were detailed to attack both north and east from Bellicourt in the direction of Bony. Some progress was made along the mound and it was discovered that the Germans had voluntarily abandoned the farm. During the night and early in the morning of 1 October, the 33rd Battalion advanced on Bony. Germans were seen to be evacuating the village and shortly after, the northern end of the tunnel was secured. The reserve brigade of the 18th Division relieved 37 Brigade near Vendhuile and outposts were established on the canal bank. The Australians in Bony pushed north and met up with units of 55 Brigade in Macquincourt Valley. This final advance had eventually come as something of a surprise. The relief of the 27th US Division by the Australians during 1 October certainly eased the problems. The Americans had fought hard and well, with several individuals winning a Medal of Honour for their bravery. It seems that many did not want to be relieved and contrived to stay with their Australian friend for a further two days. Their inexperience had unfortunately cost them dear and the real motive behind the German decision to abandon Gillemont Farm was a consequence of the Australian penetration of the valleys either side. However, the essential key to their success was the 46th Division's achievement further south. In an attempt to keep their line intact, the Germans withdrew to their next defensive position, the Le Catelet-Nauroy line. The North Midlanders and their comrades in the 32nd and

50th Divisions were to have more hard fighting in and around Gouy and Magny before they broke through into relatively open country.

Once the mopping-up operation was completed, Australian and US engineers explored the length of the Bellicourt canal tunnel. Major Lawson, the Water Supply Officer of the Australian Corps, and Captain Humphries of 105th Engineer Regiment, travelled the length of the tunnel sketching and measuring.[5] As they progressed towards the northern end, signs of bitter fighting became more apparent. Sections of the towpath and arch walls were badly damaged, several exits were demolished and walls and water seepage tunnels blown in. This prevented exploration of many chambers and cavities, from which, the officers reported, 'disagreeable odours originated'. Their strangest discovery, though, came at the southern entrance.

In a room above the arch which had originally been designed to house the machinery for the tunnel gates, the two officers found

One of the 19 concealed exits from the canal tunnel. Note the track of a light railway. IWM Q49808

several iron pots suspended from a cradle, three feet above the floor. Beneath each of the pots was the remains of a fire. Six dead Germans were piled beside the pots and, on investigation, one of the receptacles was seen to contain the cropped head of a red-haired soldier. The gruesome object was floating in a foul liquid. Two other pots contained what was described as a dirty white grease with a consistency somewhat less dense than lard. The machine room was almost dark, the only light emanating from candles carried by the two explorers and from a small hole in the ceiling. Pausing only long enough to take in the general view and ruffle with a stick the hair of the unfortunate German, the two men left.

Fuelled by contemporary propaganda of German atrocities, the officers believed they had stumbled upon a rendering plant. The liquid in the pots was melted flesh and the bodies of the dead were piled up awaiting disposal; the process had clearly been hastily abandoned when the Allied attack began. Lawson and Humphries requested that a further examination of the  machine room be made. Intelligence officers did subsequently investigate, and came to a different conclusion. They decided that, far from the room being a cadaver factory, it was a cookhouse. A high-velocity shell had penetrated the tunnel roof where the earth covering was thin – hence the hole in the ceiling – and had exploded inside the room. The blast had killed the occupants, and managed to pot the decapitated head of one victim into the suspended receptacle. The walls of the room were seen to be peppered with shell fragments and smeared with bits of bodies. A photograph taken at the time also claimed to reveal the marks of rifling made by the shell as it pierced the concrete roof.

Meanwhile, the battle moved on. Very bitter fighting was to be experienced around Prospect Hill and Estrées; Mons and 11 November were still a long way off. The protagonists were relieved by marginally

126

The grisly scene which greeted Major Lawson and Captain Humphries when they entered the 'cadaver factory' at the tunnel's southern end. IWM E3491

fresher divisions and the advance rolled on. To allow for the reconstruction of roads, huge gaps were torn through the wire of the Hindenburg Line and its trenches filled in. Bodies were collected for burial, new supplies and reinforcements followed through in the wake of the advancing brigades. Like the 46th Division to the south, the Australians and Americans had achieved a notable and remarkable victory.

Notes

1. C.Bean, *Official History of Australia in the War of 1914-1918*, Vol.VI. p.985
2. Ibid
3. G.Nichols, op.cit. p.427
4. Bean, op.cit. p.995
5. Report of the St Quentin Canal Tunnel. WO.95.451

Bellicourt and Bony today

Bellicourt sits astride the N44 and suffers as a consequence. Despite the flashing warning lights, wagons rattle through the village at unnerving speeds. The war memorial, the *Mairie* and its little square front the road. Opposite is the D331 to Hargicourt. This passes along Buckshot Ravine, passing Bellicourt British Cemetery. There are a number of German concrete shelters and machine gun posts in and around the village. Its water tower, sitting on the ridge above the disused station offers good views across to Malakoff and Ruby Woods.

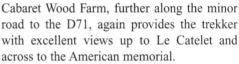

The chapel of the US Cemetery contains the names of 333 missing American soldiers. Its exterior is almost Stalinist in its starkness. Above the door is engraved: 'Those who died for their country'.

Cabaret Wood Farm, further along the minor road to the D71, again provides the trekker with excellent views up to Le Catelet and across to the American memorial.

Bony is an isolated collection of houses near a church and restaurant. The road from Hargicourt joins at the centre, with the N44 passing half a mile to the east. There is a small stone cross of unknown origin on the east bank of the crossroads of the N44 and the D442. **(6)** The old road from Bony to Bellicourt has been ploughed out but a German bunker can be reached within 600m south of the village crossroads. **(8)** Now used as something of a dump, it commands excellent views down to the US cemetery. It might have been the garrison of this pill box

Looking east from the US memorial, this photo shows the dominant position of Cabaret Wood Farm. Until it was finally out-flanked by the Australians, the garrison of this German 'tank fort' swept the ground between it and the tunnel mound with murderous machine-gun and artillery fire.

The US Cemetery at Bony. The photograph is taken from the site of the German pill box 600m south of the village and shows its excellent field of fire down the slope to the junction of the Hargicourt and Gillemont Farm roads.

which knocked out the Whippets and armoured cars on 29 September. Bony's war memorial **(7)** lists its fallen sons and also mentions 'leurs camarades Américains' lying in Bony Cemetery.

The American memorial on the N44 between Bellenglise and Bellicourt sits above the canal mound. It has a useful map and orientation table. Panoramic views across the ground attacked by the two divisions can be obtained from the platform. Reliefs adorn the monument which is set within manicured gardens and the route of the tunnel is easily traced to the north and south by the line of trees. Vauban Valley, with its dead ground for German gun batteries, lies between the mound and the N44.

Tour of Bellicourt
(Tour Map 6)
10.7kms, 6.7miles. 2.5 hours

Park at Bellicourt *Mairie*. Walk up the D93 towards Nauroy and turn left at the crossroads after 200m. After 400m bear slightly left at a crucifix and walk beside the former railway loading bays. Follow the track of the old railway beneath the water tower until it joins the N44. Turn right and walk up to the US memorial.

Return to the N44 and turn right. 200m down, an area of open rough ground leads to the tunnel mound. Cross this and follow the track across the field until it comes to a dead end. The roof of a German bunker can sometimes be seen where the tracks join. **(1)** Originally, the old road to Bony went right but this has now disappeared. Turn left and

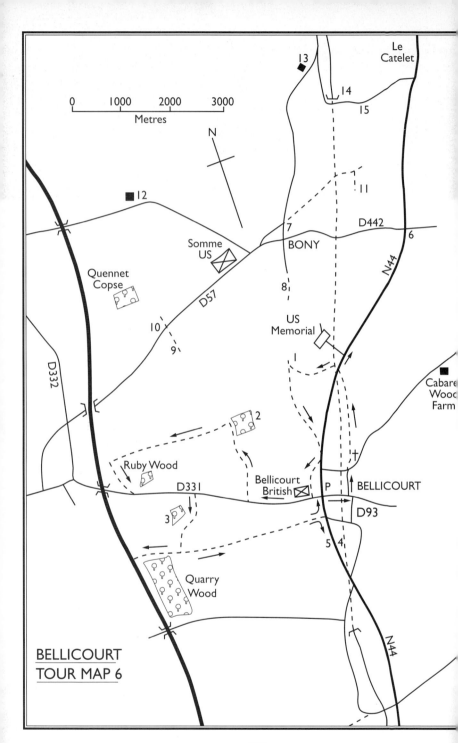

Le Catelet

13

14

15

0 1000 2000 3000
Metres

N

12

D442

6

7

BONY

N44

Somme
US

Quennet
Copse

D57

8

10

9

US Memorial

I

D332

Cabaret
Wood
Farm

2

Ruby Wood

D331

Bellicourt
British

P

BELLICOURT

3

D93

5 4

Quarry
Wood

N44

BELLICOURT
TOUR MAP 6

A recently excavated German pill box above the tunnel's southern end.

follow the track down to rejoin the N44 north of Bellicourt. In summer this track can be fairly hard going. Just as the houses of Bellicourt begin, take a small road to the right and follow it round to the D331(the Hargicourt road) and Bellicourt British Cemetery.

Walk towards Hargicourt and turn right up a track after 800m. This climbs the slope of Mount Olympus and, while often you cannot get any further than a bank to the south of Malakoff Wood, it is worth a walk up to get a perspective of the ground over which the Americans and Australians advanced in September. If the crops are down it is possible to walk on to Malakoff Wood **(2)**, following its western face to the track which joins it at its north-western corner. Quennemont Farm was in the trees with the mast across the field to the north. Turn left onto the track which runs towards the motorway. It turns left where the ruins of the sugar factory stood in 1917 and climbs up to the D331.

Turn left towards Bellicourt and after 400m take a track on the right. This initially falls away into Buckshot Ravine before climbing up past the eastern face of Diamond Wood. **(3)** At the T-junction past the wood, turn right to walk 400m along the northern face of Quarry Wood. The wood is private and, although this northern section is relatively safe, the southern half contains several dangerous workings.

Retrace your steps, continuing past the track from Diamond Wood.

The field of fire enjoyed by the machine-gunners of the pill box in the previous photo. They could fire over the heads of their comrades in the forward trenches and were supported by crews in other similar boxes on the slopes to both left and right. The trees at the far end of Quarry Ravine are those which surround the rebuilt sugar factory near Ruby Farm.

This is Sentinel Ridge and offers good views down Quarry Ravine. Follow the track down to Bellicourt. A light railway followed the ravine and circled round immediately south of where your track ends to cling to the valley. It turned east before the tunnel mouth and continued on to Nauroy. Turn right at the bottom of the track from Sentinel Ridge and follow the grass until it crosses the stream. Walk up to the main road (N44). Just south of the large farm opposite is a white wall on the east side of the N44. Some German bunkers are in the field beyond. **(4)** On the west side of the road, 20m north of the 'Parking' sign, another bunker is buried in a patch of nettles and ivy. **(5)** Return to the car at the *Mairie.*

Tour of Bony
10.8kms, 6.75miles

This route is easy to do by car. Begin at Bony crossroads. 600m down the small road from the crossroads heading south is a German pill box. **(8)** Return to the crossroads and turn left onto the D57. Visit the American cemetery.

On the crest of the hill 1500m further down the D57, the mast on the left marks the site of Quennemont Farm **(9)**, while immediately opposite on the other side of the D57 is the 'Five Ways'. **(10)** Park on the 'Five Ways' to get good views to Quennet Copse and across the motorway to the high ground beyond. Facing you on that slope were Artaxerxes, Rifleman and Benjamin Posts. Return to Bony and take the small left fork off the main road into the village. It joins the D57 running between Bony and Vendhuile. A good walk begins at this crossroads. Walk north along the track to the canal mound. Cross it and after 400m it turns right. Originally the track ran down to Le Catelet but it is now overgrown. Follow the track to the right which stops at Bony Point. **(11)** This position gives fine panoramic views to the north, east and south.

Return to the D57 and head towards Vendhuile. Gillemont Farm is on the crest to the left **(12)**, with Claymore Valley also running in from the same direction. At Macquincourt Farm **(13)** turn sharp right towards Le Catelet. Park on the verge above the tunnel and walk down through the trees to the northern end. **(14)**

Continue on towards Le Catelet. The high ground to the Knob **(15)** is on your right. Turn right onto the N44 and follow the road down to Bellicourt. Vauban Valley is on the right of the road.

Chapter Eight

SELECTED CEMETERIES IN THE EPEHY AREA
(The plot, row and grave number are given for various individuals)

Bellicourt British Cemetery

This cemetery lies 100 yards to the west of the main village crossroads. It was begun in September 1918 when 73 dead of the 46th and Australian Divisions were buried in what is now Plot 1. It now contains members of the 35th and 59th Divisions from April and May 1917 and a substantial number of men from the 66th Division of March 1918. There are two special memorials, neat squares of a dozen headstones enclosing a collection of bushes and shrubs, to men of the 1/North Staffordshire and the 2/4th Ox & Bucks killed near Maissemy. These men are 'believed' to be or 'known' to be buried among the unidentified graves. There are also a number of 1st Division men killed near Pontruet and Gricourt in September 1918. These include Second Lieutenant Sir John Bridge Shiffner, 6th Bart, of the 2/Sussex (V.E.5) and Second Lieutenant Charles Wake of 2/KRRC, the son of Admiral Sir Drury St Aubyn Wake.(VI.A.6) Several others of the 2/Sussex who were killed on 24 September lie in Berthaucourt Communal. There are also a number of the 5/Leicester killed at Pontruet on 24 September. These men were originally buried at Ste Hélêne, but after the war about two dozen of them, along with several of the 2/Sussex, were reinterred at Cerisy-Gailly Military Cemetery. Others of the Leicester Regiment were taken the shorter distance to Bellicourt for reburial.

Lieutenant-Colonel Bernard Vann VC, MC and Bar is also buried at Bellicourt. (II.O.1) He won his VC for rallying his battalion near Bellenglise on 29 September and was killed four days later near Ramicourt, once again leading from the front. At the far end is another Forester, Sergeant Reg Ford of the 1/5th Battalion who had won the DCM and MM. (VI.L.2) There are also over 300 Australians, many of whom were killed during the slog through Hargicourt and Ascension Valley, or as they attacked towards Bellicourt.

The headstone of Lieutenant-Colonel Vann VC in Bellicourt British Cemetery.

Domino British Cemetery

South of Vaucellette Farm is Domino Cemetery. A small, rather exposed cemetery lying west of the railway, it contains a mixture of regiments among its 51 graves. It took its name from the 33rd Division's sign and was made in early October. There are several 2/Argyll & Sutherland Highlanders and 2/Worcester. Four officers of the Cameronians (Scottish Rifles) killed on 21 September lie next to each other. Many of their men killed on the same day were buried in Meath Cemetery. Another officer lies in Plot II.

Epéhy Communal Cemetery

The communal cemetery on the south-east side of Epéhy includes the grave of one British soldier and a mass grave of five villagers shot by the Germans in 1914. Lieutenant Robert Herman of the 2/5 South Lancashire Regiment and the RFC was buried by the Germans in September 1916. Herman, of 19 Squadron, was flying a BE12 and there is some dispute as to who actually shot him down. It was either *Offizier Stellvertreter* L.Reimann of *Jasta 2* (the unit where many future aces, including von Richtofen, cut their teeth) or *Leutnant* R.Berthold, the 'Iron Knight'. After the war Berthold met an unusual death when German communists used the ribbon of his *Pour le Merité* to strangle him.

Epéhy Wood Farm Cemetery

On the road to Saulcourt is Epéhy Wood Farm Cemetery. Plots I and II were made by the 12th Division following the capture of the village in September 1918. They largely contain men of the 9/RF, 7/Sussex and 9/Essex. These are close-packed rows, the closeness of the headstones indicates the haste with which the dead were buried. The remaining plots were concentrated from other cemeteries. Most of them contained soldiers of the 12th and 58th Divisions, although Epéhy RE Cemetery, in the field to the north of the existing one, contained soldiers killed between April and December 1917. Several of these were killed during the raids by the 35th Division in August 1917. There are also men of the 42nd and 48th Divisions killed during April and May 1917. There are a number of identified men of 110 (Leicestershire) Brigade killed between December and February and no doubt a good deal more of them among the 234 unknown graves. In total there are just under 1000 graves.

Among the fallen officers are Lieutenant Leonard Forbes of the 6/Essex who, as a private, survived the London Scottish's defence of

Messines Ridge on Halloween 1914, (I.E.11) and the crew of an AWFK8 shot down near May Copse while on artillery observation in February 1918. The pilot, Second Lieutenant Humphrey Wilson RFC, had returned from the Malay States to enlist. (V.D.13) Another man who travelled some way to fight on the Western Front was Lieutenant Eynaud, KO Malta Regiment. He was attached to D Company of the 2/Munster. (III.E.17)

Fins New British Cemetery

Over 1200 British and nearly 300 Germans lie together in this substantial open cemetery. The village was occupied by British troops in April 1917 and, at first, the local churchyard was used for burials. The British cemetery was begun in July 1917, and was used largely by the 9th, 40th and 61st Divisions. Many of the 40th Division were killed or died of wounds following their attack on Welsh and Fusilier Ridges near Villers-Plouich in April 1917. Eight men of the 57th Coy Labour Corps were killed during an air raid in January 1918 and are buried here. (IV.A) There are also a number of Guards who were killed during their attack on Gonnelieu and Gauche Wood. By the time the Germans forced their way through the defences of the 6/KOSB and the staff of the South African Brigade on 23 March, there were nearly 600 graves in the cemetery. The Germans then buried their dead and also those British who died in their hands. The 33rd Division used it again in September 1918 and after the war nearly 600 graves were brought in from the churchyard and elsewhere. Captain Eric Molyneux of the Worcestershire Regiment, attached to III Corps Cyclist Battalion is buried here. (II.E.10) He was presumably a member of the scratch force assembled by 12th Division to defend Révelon Ridge on 30 November 1917.

Gauche Wood Cemetery

The Cross of Sacrifice in Gauche Wood Cemetery can be seen easily from Villers-Guislain Communal Cemetery and is approached by a small lane running west from the village. The cemetery is of an unusual layout: the two rows of headstones are very close together, with the stones set alternately. It is a small, compact cemetery, beautifully framed by its arboreal backdrop. The cemetery was made by the 21st Division's Burial Officer in early October, although most of the graves (largely 7/Border, 7/Lincoln and 10/West Yorks) are those of the 17th Division.

Heudicourt Communal and Extension Cemeteries

There are four British soldiers buried in the communal cemetery. One of the three lying in the small plot the left hand side near the main entrance is Private David Ross, 2nd South African Regiment. Ross died of wounds on 25 March 1918, aged 14 and 3 months – quite possibly the youngest 'British' soldier killed in the Great War. He had previously been wounded at Passchendaele in 1917. Two other men, who also presumably died of wounds while in German hands, are buried in graves alongside, while the fourth man, Lance-Corporal Larcombe of the 2/Devon, was buried by the British.

The extension is a pretty little cemetery, shaded by four large trees, and contains 85 graves. A good proportion of these are men of the 6/KOSB. Sixteen of them were killed on 16 December 1917. The battalion was not engaged in any real fighting during the period, and spent most of its time attempting to keep the trenches in some sort of repair. According to the brigadier of 27 Brigade, they 'burrowed into that chalk like beavers'.(1) Lieutenant-Colonel Malcolm Docherty, DSO and Lieutenant-Colonel Edwin Corbyn, Commanding Officers of the Lord Strathcona's Horse and 18/Lancers respectively, lie together. (C.6.7) They were both killed on 1 December during the cavalry's counter-attack near Gauche Wood.

Lempire Communal Cemetery

The cemetery contains some Gloucesters and Berkshires of the 48th Division and eight 19/DLI who were killed during a German raid on Rifleman Post on 20 July 1917. One soldier of the North Staffs died as a PoW and was buried by the Germans.

Meath Cemetery

This isolated little cemetery was also made by the 33rd Division. It contains 122 soldiers, mainly of the 1/Cameronians and 1/Queen's from the 21 September. There are also many 2/10 London of the 58th Division. Having lost its two trees in recent years, the cemetery now looks rather stark. From its commanding position, three other British cemeteries can be seen.

Pigeon Ravine Cemetery

This beautiful little collection of graves, often almost enclosed by swaying stems of maize, lies west of the motorway on the C5. It was made by the 33rd Division's Burial Officer in early October 1918 and contains the remains of 135 men. The eight officers of the 2/Worcester, killed during the diversionary attack on 29 September lie in a separate plot against the boundary wall. The remainder rest in three rows and contain 74 other Worcesters who fell that day in Gloster Road, Queen Victoria's, Rangers, Queens and KRRCs. This is a good example not only of a battlefield cemetery but also one which contains a high proportion of known graves. It demonstrates the sizable number of men, from a limited number of battalions, who could be killed in a single day within a confined area. Those who died a little to the north on the same day, were buried in Meath Cemetery. The cross of this cemetery can be identified on the crest of the spur to the north-west.

Ronssoy Communal Cemetery

The communal cemetery contains a total of 45 British burials. The old register explains that eight soldiers were buried by the Germans. It is difficult to identify these as only one, Private Murrell of the 7/Queen's, has a date of death when the village was in German hands. There are six 6/Connaught Rangers and the battalion MO of late December 1917 and the rest are those who fell in September and October 1918. These lie in a separate plot at the southern end. There are many 25/Royal Welch Fusiliers, MGC and 7/Bedfords of 18-22 September 1918. There are also five Australian Pioneers killed on 29 September. These men were some of those responsible for extending the roads towards Bellicourt and Bony. There is an untidy plot of French soldiers near the east fence.

Saulcourt Churchyard Extension

Another infrequently visited little cemetery which has an attractive surround and layout. It can be reached via the churchyard or by the lane which runs beside the church. There are 95 British graves and seven German. It was begun by the 48th Division in April 1917 and used until September of the following year. Two of the earliest graves are those of Captain Stafford and Second Lieutenant Harrison, MC, of the 6/Warwick. (B.2.3) The Germans buried men of the Leicestershire Brigade who fell during the defence of Epéhy, as well as some Manchesters, East Yorks and Irish of the 16th Division. There are also some Londoners of September 1918.

Somme US Cemetery

The American Cemetery has an impressive entrance, which couples as the memorial chapel, and is always well-maintained. Bare, and

The crosses of US Medal of Honor winners, such as Lieutenant Turner in the Somme Cemetery, have their lettering highlighted with gold paint and the addition of a star.

lacking the variety of plants common in British cemeteries, it contains the graves of 1837 men and a memorial to 333 missing. Among the graves are three men who served with British units. They include Lieutenant Theodore Hostetter, killed in September 1918 while flying with the RAF, and Lieutenant James Hall of 60 Squadron, killed on the opening day of the Battle of Amiens. Hall had failed the height limit of the US Air Service and instead joined the RFC. On 8 August he was flying a SE5A behind the German lines near Foucaucourt. Lothar von Richtofen shot him down and the aircraft disintegrated as it hit the ground. Hall was originally buried near Maricourt and reinterred after the war.

The graves of 128 unidentified soldiers in the cemetery carry a variation of Kipling's 'Known unto God'. The US crosses have: "Here rests an honored American Soldier. Known but to God'.

Ste Emilie Valley British Cemetery

The Germans buried British dead of March 1918 in three mass graves. They are largely men of the 16th (Irish) Division, including several Pioneers who fought alongside the infantry in the defence of Ste Emilie. Post-war concentration of September graves and of men of the 59th Division now fill the other plots. These include troops of the 1/Herts and 11/Sussex, two battalions which were rushed up to Ste Emilie on 21 March. The September graves are mostly Yeomanry of the 74th Division. Sergeant William Milton of the 16th (Royal 1st

Nestled in the valley a few hundred yards south of the modern sugar refinery at Ste Emilie, lies the British cemetery with its dead of 1918.

Devon and North Devon Yeomanry), who had fought in Gallipoli, Egypt and Palestine and held the TF Efficiency Medal, was one of the several men of his battalion killed near here on 10 September. (II.D.15) 222 of the graves are unnamed.

Targelle Ravine Cemetery

Lying a little to the west of the motorway, this unusual cemetery would have been better named Glasgow Highlanders Cemetery. 76 of the 114 burials were from the 9/HLI killed on 29 September 1918. There are two long rows with cross rows between. The remainder of the burials are mainly from the 6/Cameronians and 1/Wiltshire.

Unicorn British Cemetery

The cemetery was begun by the 50th Division, burying men of the 18th who fell in September 1918. These men lie in Plot I. The other plots were created by concentration following the armistice. Two of the largest battlefield cemeteries which gave up their dead for Unicorn were made in Bassè Boulogne. La Paurelle British was begun by the 1/5 Gloucester immediately after they took the hamlet in April 1917. Today, Unicorn holds 768 known British and Dominion soldiers, 409 unknown and four Indians. Corporal Lawrence Weathers of the 43rd Australian Battalion died of wounds received during the attack on the Hindenburg Line on 29 September. (III.C.5) Weathers had won the VC at Péronne earlier in the month. Lieutenant-Colonel Hindle DSO, 1/4 LNL, who was killed leading his battalion against Villers-Guislain, is buried here, (IV.G.9) and so is Lieutenant-Colonel Scott DSO, of the 2/RIR. (II.E.23) As we might expect, there is a substantial number of known and unknown men of Scott's division, the 16th, as well as soldiers from the East Lancs and the Lancashire Fusiliers who died on the same day. There are a few cavalry, including a group of Queen's Own Oxfordshire Hussars killed on 21 June 1917, but the majority of the dead are those of the Essex, Northants, West Kents and East Surreys of the 18th Division.

Unicorn Cemetery lies immediately west of a modern motorway near Lempire. Corporal Weathers VC was buried here after dying of wounds in late September 1918.

Villers-Faucon Communal and Extension Cemeteries

The communal cemetery has over 220 British and 90 German graves from 1917. These include the officers of the 1/6 Gloucester who were killed when their HQ was destroyed by a delayed action device in April 1917, Second Lieutenants Dunville (A.21) and Parsons (A.16), both VC winners, and Brigadier-General Ormsby, CB, commander of 127 Brigade, who was killed at Catelet Copse. (D.41) There are also many men of the 35th Division killed or died of wounds during their attacks on Gillemont Farm and the Knoll.

The extension was also begun in April 1917 and contains 453 British and 66 German graves. Major F.Atkinson, DSO, and Major Arthur Fraser, DSO, both squadron commanders of 9th Hodson's Horse are buried here. (A.16,17) They were killed near Gauche Wood on 30 November. There are also several Indian cavalry of the Central India Horse who were killed a day later in Catelet Valley, and a number of Guards who died of wounds following their advance near Villers-Guislain. The 16th Division used it as one of its cemeteries while line-holding at Lempire in early 1918.

Villers-Guislain Communal Cemetery

600m to the west of Villers-Guislain lies its communal cemetery. At the far end is a plot of 50 British graves. Many of them are from the 35th Division – 23/Manchester and 18/LF – although nine are from the 2/Cameronians (Scottish Rifles) killed on 5 May 1917. Eighteen men whose graves were later lost are represented by a special memorial.

Villers Hill Cemetery

Like Meath and Pigeon Ravine Cemeteries, Villers Hill was made by the 33rd Division's Burial Officer. It was originally known as Middlesex Cemetery. Fifty of the regiment's 1st Battalion and 35 of the 2/Argyll & Sutherland Highlanders lie in the close-packed rows of Plot 1. There was a great deal of concentration after the armistice and the cemetery now contains 1066 graves from a large variety of regiments. There are a few men of the 2/Devon, one of the first battalions into the village of Villers-Guislain in April 1917, some Lord Strathcona's Horse, Guards and Loyal North Lancashires of 30 November - 1 December 1917 and Northumberland Fusiliers killed near Vaucellette Farm on 21 March. The majority however, are from those battalions which repeatedly attacked the village and its outlying fields in September 1918.

Note

1. S.Gillon, *The KOSB in the Great War,* p.358

BIBLIOGRAPHY

C.Atkinson, *The Queen's Own Royal West Kent,* (London, 1929)
C.Bean, *Official History of Australia in the Great War,* (Sydney, 1943)
J.Bickersteth, *History of the 6th Cavalry Brigade,* (Baynard, n.d.)
J.Boraston & C.Bax, *The Eight Division in war, 1914-1918,* (Medici, 1926)
H.Davson, *The History of the 35th Division in the Great War,* (Sifton, 1926)
J.Ewing, *The History of the 9th (Scottish) Division 1914-1919,* (Murray, 1921)
A.Keith-Falconer, *The Oxforshire Hussars in the Great War,* (Murray, 1927)
F.Fox, *The Royal Inniskilling Fusiliers,* (London, 1928)
S.Geoghegan, *The Campaigns and History of the Royal Irish Regiment, Vol.2,* (Blackwood, 1927)
F.Gibbon, *The 42nd (East Lancashire) Division 1914-1918,* (Country Life, 1920)
S.Gillon, *The KOSB in the Great War,* (Nelson & Sons)
W.Grey, *The 2nd City of London Regiment in the Great War,* (HQ, 1929)
A.Horne, *The Diary of a World War 1 Cavalry Officer,* (IWM Dept. of Documents)
G.Hutchinson, *The Thirty-Third Division in France & Flanders,* (Waterlow, 1921)
L.Lumley, *The Eleventh Hussars,* (RUSI, 1936)
J.Lunt, *The Scarlet Lancers,* (Leo Cooper, 1993)
M.Middlebrook, *The Kaiser's Battle,* (Penguin, 1983)
K.Mitchinson, *Pioneer Battalions in the Great War,* (Leo Cooper, 1997)
G.Nichols, *The 18th Division in the Great War,* (Blackwood1922)
P.Oldham, *The Hindenburg Line,* (Leo Cooper, 1997)
F.Petre, *The Royal Berkshire Regiment, Vol.2*
C.Potter & A.Fothergill, *The History of the the 2/6th Lancashire Fusiliers,* (1927)
H.Powell & J.Edwards, *The Sussex Yeomanry & 16th Bn, Royal Sussex Regiment,* (Melrose, 1921)
A.Scott & P.Brumwell, *The History of the 12th Division,* (Nisbet, 1923)
J.Shakespear, *The Thirty-Fourth Division,* (Witherby, 1921)
C.Simpson, *The History of the Lincolnshire Regiment,* (London, 1931)
H.Stacke, *The Worcester Regiment in the Great War,* (Cheshire & Sons, 1929)
E. Vaughan, *Some Desperate Glory,* (Warne, 1981)
C.Ward, *The 74th (Yeomanry) Division in Syria and France,* (John Murray, 1922)
R.Woollcombe, *The First Tank Battle,* (Barker, 1967)
P.Wright, *The First Buckinghamshire Battalion,* (Hazell, 1920)
F.Whitmore, *The 10th PWO Royal Hussars & Essex Yeomanry,* (Benham, 1920)
H.Wylly, *The 1st and 2nd Battalions of the Leicester Regiment,*
H.Wylly, *The Border Regiment in the Great War,* (Gale & Polden, 1921)
H.Wylly, *Crown and Company,* (Gale & Polden, n.d.)
E.Wyrall, *The Gloucester Regiment in the War,* (Methuen, 1931)
E.Wyrall, *The East Yorkshire Regiment in the Great War,*
The 59th Division, 1915-1918. Various authors, (Chesterfield, 1928)
The Official History of the Great War, France and Belgium. Various authors, (HMSO)
The Marquess of Anglesey, *A History of the British Cavalry 1816-1919,* (Leo Cooper, 1997)

Selective Index